SECON
EDITIO

Volume II

ISBN-13: 978-1-4234-2452-9
ISBN-10: 1-4234-2452-2

7777 W. Bluemound Rd. P.O. Box 13819 Milwaukee, WI 53213

For all works contained herein:
Unauthorized copying, arranging, adapting, recording or public performance is an infringement of copyright.
Infringers are liable under the law.

Visit Hal Leonard Online at
www.halleonard.com

PREFACE

The Real Book is the answer to the fake book. It is an alternative to the plethora of poorly designed, illegible, inaccurate, badly edited volumes which abound on the market today. The Real Book is extremely accurate, neat, and is designed, above all, for practical use. Every effort has been made to make it enjoyable to play. Here are some of the primary features:

1. FORMAT

a. The book is professionally copied and meticulously checked for accuracy in melody, harmony, and rhythms.

b. Form within each tune, including both phrases and larger sections, is clearly delineated and placed in obvious visual arrangement.

c. All two-page tunes open to face one another.

d. Most standard-type tunes remain true to their original harmonies with little or no reharmonization. The exceptions include a handful of jazz interpretations of popular songs and Broadway showtunes, as well as some modifications using modern notation and variation among turnarounds.

2. SELECTION OF TUNES AND EDITING

a. Major jazz composers of the last 60 years are highlighted, with special attention given to the 1960s and 1970s.

b. While some commonly played tunes are absent from the book, many of the classics are here, including bop standards and a fine selection of Duke Ellington masterpieces. See Real Book volumes 1 and 3 for more tunes.

c. Many of the included arrangements represent the work of the jazz giants of the last 40 years – Miles, Coltrane, Shorter, Hancock, Rollins, Silver, and Monk, as well as a variety of newer artists.

d. A variety of recordings and alternate editions were consulted to create the most accurate and user-friendly representations of the tunes, whether used in a combo setting or as a solo artist.

3. SOURCE REFERENCE

a. The composer(s) of every tune is listed.

b. Every song presented in the Real Book is now fully licensed for use.

Second Edition

This new edition contains tunes that are re-arranged, re-transcribed and most importantly, licensed, so that you may study and play these works more accurately and legally. Enjoy!

C Cont.

D

E

F

G

H

L Cont.

M

N

O

P

Q

R

R Cont.

S

T

U

W

Y

ABLUTION

-LENNIE TRISTANO

(♩=192 (MED. UP))

Copyright © 1980 C & C Jazz, a division of the Lennie Tristano Jazz Foundation, Inc.

Copyright © 1968 MIYAKO MUSIC
Copyright Renewed
All Rights Administered by IRVING MUSIC, INC.

Copyright © 1975 J & H Publishing Company (ASCAP)
Copyright Renewed
All Rights Administered by Stollman & Stollman o/b/o J & H Publishing Company

Copyright © 1941 by Regent Music Corporation (BMI)
Copyright Renewed by Ragbag Music Publishing Corporation (ASCAP), Regent Music Corporation (BMI) and Rytvoc Music, Inc. (ASCAP)
All Rights for Ragbag Music Publishing Corporation Controlled and Administered by Jewel Music Publishing Co., Inc.

ALFIE'S THEME

-SONNY ROLLINS

(SWING)

Copyright © 1966 (Renewed 1995) by Ensign Music Corporation

Copyright © 1959, 1961 by Edward B. Marks Music Company
Copyright Renewed

Copyright © 1941 FRANCE MUSIC CORP. and CHAPPELL & CO.
Copyright Renewed
All Rights for FRANCE MUSIC CORP. in English Speaking Countries Controlled and Administered by
UNIVERSAL MUSIC CORP.

ALTO ITIS

-OLIVER E. NELSON

(UP)

Bbmaj7 B°7 C-7 C#°7 D-7 G7 C-7 F7

Bb7 Eb7 Ab7 1. Bb G7 C-7 F7

2. Bb F7 Bb D7

G7 C7

F7 Bbmaj7 B°7 C-7 C#°7

D-7 G7 C-7 F7 Bb7 Eb7 Ab7

Bb7 F7 Bb

Copyright © 1961 (Renewed) Noslen Music Co. L.L.C.

© 1976 (Renewed 2004) JOBETE MUSIC CO., INC. and BLACK BULL MUSIC
c/o EMI APRIL MUSIC INC.

Dmaj7
E-7
A7
Dmaj7
F#-7
B7
Emaj7
C#7
F#-7
G#7
C#7sus4
C#7b9
F#-7
E7
Dmaj7
C#-7
B-7
C#7#9
F#-7

APRIL SKIES

(MED. UP)

— BUDDY COLLETTE

Copyright © 1999 Prestige Music

Gmaj7 A-7 B-7 C7
G-7 C7 G-7 C7
A-7 D7 B-7 E7
A-7 D7 Gmaj7 E7 A-7 D7
AFTER SOLOS, D.C. AL
Gmaj9

ARE YOU HAVIN' ANY FUN?

(BRIGHT)

-SAMMY FAIN/JACK YELLEN

Copyright © 1939 by Chappell & Co. and Fain Music Co.
Copyright Renewed

Copyright © 1978 by Thelonious Music Corp.

Copyright © 1952 by Peer International Corporation
Copyright Renewed

AVALON

(MED. UP)

- VINCENT ROSE / AL JOLSON / B.G. DESYLVA

Copyright © 2005 by HAL LEONARD CORPORATION

Copyright © 1937 (Renewed 1964) by Famous Music Corporation in the U.S.A.
Rights outside the U.S.A. Controlled by EMI Mills Music Inc. and Warner Bros. Publications U.S. Inc.

(MED. BLUES)

BA-LUE BOLIVAR BA-LUES-ARE

(BOLIVAR BLUES)

-THELONIOUS MONK

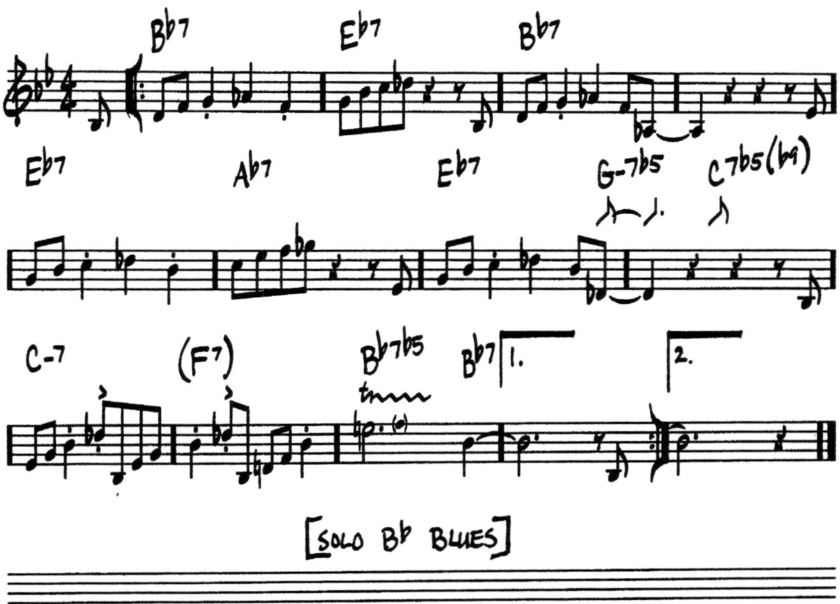

Copyright © 1958 (Renewed 1986) by Thelonious Music Corp.

BABY, IT'S COLD OUTSIDE

(MED.)

-FRANK LOESSER

Fmaj7 F#o7 G-7 C7 G-7 C7

Fmaj7 D-7 C-7 F7

B♭maj7 1. B♭-7 E♭7

Fmaj7 D-7 G7 C7

2. G7 C7 Fmaj7 A-7♭5 D7

G7 C7 F6 (C7)

CAN ALSO BE PLAYED "CALL AND RESPONSE" STYLE WITH ADDITIONAL MELODY INSTRUMENT

© 1948 (Renewed) FRANK MUSIC CORP.

Copyright © 1961 (Renewed 1989) by MJQ Music, Inc.

BAGS' GROOVE

(MED. SWING)

—MILT JACKSON

© Copyright 1958 (Renewed 1986) Reecie Music

Copyright © 1949 by Richard Rodgers and Oscar Hammerstein II
Copyright Renewed
WILLIAMSON MUSIC owner of publication and allied rights throughout the world

Copyright © 1956 (Renewed 1984) Criterion Music Corp.

Dbmaj7 E-7 A7 D-7 G7b9 Cmaj7
C#-7 F#7#9 Bmaj7 E-7 A7#5 G-7b5 F#-7 B7b9
E-7 A7b9 F#-7 B7b9 E-7 G-6 F#-7 F°7
E-7 A7b9 Dmaj7
(ENDING)
D-7 G7 E-7 A7#9 D7b9 Ab7 Ab°7 A°7 Bb°7 B°7 C Dbmaj9 Cmaj9

BALTIMORE ORIOLE

- Hoagy Carmichael / Paul Francis Webster

(MED. BALLAD)

Copyright © 1942, 1944 by Songs Of Peer, Ltd. and Warner Bros. Inc.
Copyright Renewed

Copyright © 1948 (Renewed 1976) Atlantic Music Corp.
All Rights for the World excluding the U.S. Controlled and Administered by Screen Gems - EMI Music Inc.

Copyright © 1974 by Ecaroh Music, Inc.
Copyright Renewed 2002

(MED. SLOW DIXIELAND)

BASIN STREET BLUES

-SPENCER WILLIAMS

A N.C. Bb C-7 C#o7 Bb/D N.C.

Bb/D C#o7 C-7 F7 Bb Bb/Ab Eb/G Eb/Gb Bb/F N.C.

1. F7 2. B Bb D7

G7 C7 F7

Bb/D C#o7 C-7 F7 Bb D7

G7 Ab7 G7 C7 F7

Bb Bb7/D Eb6 Eo7 Bb/F G7b9 C-7 F7 SOLO ON B

AFTER SOLOS, D.S. AL ⊕

⊕ Bb/F F7 Bb6

© 1928, 1929, 1933 (Renewed) EDWIN H. MORRIS & COMPANY, A Division of MPL Music Publishing, Inc.

BE-BOP

-John "Dizzy" Gillespie

Copyright © 1944, 1945 UNIVERSAL MUSIC CORP.
Copyright Renewed

BETTER LEAVE IT ALONE

(MED.)

-CLIFFORD JORDAN

Copyright © 1962 Orpheum Music
Copyright Renewed

Copyright © 1945, 1946, 1947 (Renewed) by France Music Corp. and Range Road Music Inc.

Copyright © 1960 (Renewed 1988) by MJQ Music, Inc.

TRO - © Copyright 1979, 1991 and 2002 Ludlow Music, Inc., New York, NY

Copyright © 1956, 1962 by Edward B. Marks Music Company
Copyright Renewed

Copyright © 1945 (Renewed 1973) Atlantic Music Corp.
All Rights for the World excluding the U.S. Controlled and Administered by Screen Gems-EMI Music Inc.

BIRD FEATHERS

(BOP)

-CHARLIE PARKER

Bb6

Eb6 Ab7 Bb6 G7

C-7 F7 D-7 Dbo7 1. C-7 F7

2. C-7 F7 Bb6

Copyright © 1961 SONGS OF UNIVERSAL, INC.
Copyright Renewed

© 1977 (Renewed), 1978 MULATTO MUSIC

(FUNK)
(G PEDAL)
PLAY 10X
D.S. TO A, TAKE REPEATS
PLAY THROUGH C, GO TO E
REPEAT AND FADE ON E

BIRK'S WORKS

-Dizzy Gillespie

F-7 G-7b5 C7#5 F-7

C-7b5 F7#9 Bb-7 F-7

Ab-7 Db7 G-7b5 C7#5(#9)

1. F-7 2. F-7

© 1957 (Renewed 1985) DIZLO MUSIC
All Rights Controlled and Administered by EMI APRIL MUSIC INC.

(SLOW SWING) THE BIRTH OF THE BLUES

– RAY HENDERSON / B.G. DE SYLVA / LEW BROWN

Copyright © 1926 Stephen Ballentine Music, Warner Bros. Inc. and Ray Henderson Music
Copyright Renewed
All Rights for Stephen Ballentine Music Administered by The Songwriters Guild Of America

(SLOW BLUES)

BLACK AND TAN FANTASY

-DUKE ELLINGTON
BUB MILEY

Copyright © 1927 (Renewed 1954) and Assigned to Famous Music Corporation and EMI Mills Music Inc. in the U.S.A.
Rights for the world outside the U.S.A. Controlled by EMI Mills Music Inc.

(BALLAD)

BLAME IT ON MY YOUTH

- OSCAR LEVANT / EDWARD HEYMAN

Ebmaj7 F-7 | G-7 F#7b5 | F-7 E°7 | F-7 Bb7

F-7 E°7 | F-7 Bb7 | G-7 F-7 Bb7 | Ebmaj7 Eb7

Abmaj7 Bb7 | G-7 C-7 | F-7 Bb7 | Ebmaj7

D-7b5 G7b9 | C-7 | F7 B7#5 | Bb7

Ebmaj7 F-7 | G-7 F#7b5 | F-7 E°7 | F-7 Bb7

F-7 E°7 | F-7 Bb7 | G-7 F-7 Bb7 | Bb-7 Eb7

Abmaj7 Bb7 | G-7 C-7 | F-7 F-7/Eb | Db9(#11) C7

F-7 E°7 | F-7 Bb7 | Eb6 (C7b9 | F-7 Bb7)

Copyright © 1934 UNIVERSAL - POLYGRAM INTERNATIONAL PUBLISHING, INC. and OSCAR LEVANT MUSIC
Copyright Renewed
All Rights for OSCAR LEVANT MUSIC Controlled and Administered by THE SONGWRITERS GUILD OF AMERICA

BLOOMDIDO

(FAST BLUES)

-CHARLIE PARKER

Copyright © 1953 (Renewed 1981) Atlantic Music Corp.

(MED. UP BLUES)

BLOW MR. DEXTER

-DEXTER GORDON

© 1946 (Renewed 1974) SCREEN GEMS-EMI MUSIC INC.

Copyright © 1944 UNIVERSAL MUSIC CORP.
Copyright Renewed

BLUE SERGE

—MERCER ELLINGTON

Copyright © 1944 (Renewed) by Tempo Music, Inc. and Music Sales Corporation (ASCAP)
All Rights Administered by Music Sales Corporation

Copyright © 1965 Prestige Music
Copyright Renewed

BLUE SILVER

— HORACE SILVER

(MED.)

© 1967 by Ecaroh Music, Inc.
Copyright Renewed 1995

BLUE SKIES

-IRVING BERLIN

(MED.)

E- B7/D# G/D

C#-7b5 Gmaj7 E7b9 A-7 D7

G6 1. F#-7b5 B7b9 2. A-7 D7

Gmaj7 F7 Gmaj7 F7 Gmaj7

D7 Gmaj7 F7 Gmaj7 F7 Gmaj7

D7 Gmaj7 B7#5 E- B7/D#

G/D C#-7b5 Gmaj7 E7b9

A-7 D7 G6 (F#-7b5 B7b9)

FINE

© Copyright 1927 by Irving Berlin
Copyright Renewed

Copyright © 1965 Prestige Music
Copyright Renewed

BLUES FOR WOOD

(MED. FAST)

-WOODY SHAW

© 1981 MAYFLOWER MUSIC CORP.

(Bright Blues)

BLUES IN THE CLOSET

- Oscar Pettiford

© 1955 Orpheus Music, Inc.
Copyright Renewed

BLUES MARCH

(MED.)

-BENNY GOLSON

Copyright © 1958 (Renewed 1986) IBBOB MUSIC, INC. d/b/a TIME STEP MUSIC (ASCAP)

(MED. FAST)

BOHEMIA AFTER DARK

-OSCAR PETTIFORD

G- A-7b5 D7 G- A-7b5 D7

G- A-7b5 D7 G- 1. Eb7 D7 G- D7 2. (G-)

G-9/C

Eb7 D7b9

G- A-7b5 D7 G- A-7b5 D7

G- A-7b5 D7 G- Eb7 D7 G- (D7)

© 1955 Orpheus Music, Inc.
Copyright Renewed

BOOKER'S WALTZ

(JAZZ WALTZ)

- BOOKER LITTLE

Copyright © 1960 (Renewed 1988) Second Floor Music

© 1972 (Renewed 2000) COLGEMS-EMI MUSIC INC.

Copyright © 1947 (Renewed) by Music Sales Corporation (ASCAP) and Embassy Music Corporation (BMI)
All Rights outside the United States Controlled by Music Sales Corporation

C
Bbmaj7 C-7 D-7 Eb-7 D-7 G7 C-7 D7
G-7 C#o7 C-7 F7 Bbmaj7
FINE
D
D7/F# G- D7 G- Bo7 C-7 G7 C-7 Gb7
3
F7
(FILL)
B7 Bb6
(SOLO BREAK)
SOLO A B C
AFTER SOLOS, D.C. AL FINE

Copyright © 1999 Prestige Music

BRILLIANT CORNERS

–THELONIOUS MONK

1ST TIME: SLOW WALK, EVEN 8THS
ON REPEAT: MED.-UP SWING

Copyright © 1958 (Renewed 1986) by Thelonious Music Corp.

© 1956 (Renewed 1984) BEECHWOOD MUSIC CORP.

—LENNIE NIEHAUS

(MED.)

Fmaj7 A-7 Ab7 G-7 C7b9 A-7 D7#9 G-7 C7

F6 F7/A Bb B°7 F/C G7 C7 F6 N.C.

C-7 F7 Bbmaj7

Bb-7 Eb7 Abmaj7 G-7 C7

Fmaj7 A-7 Ab7 G-7 C7b9 A-7 D7#9 G-7 C7

F6 F7/A Bb B°7 F/C G7 C7 F6 (SOLO BREAK)

FINE

Copyright © 1955 Contemporary Music
Copyright Renewed

© 1958 (Renewed 1986) EMI LONGITUDE MUSIC

(MED. UP)

BYE BYE BLACKBIRD

-RAY HENDERSON/MORT DIXON

Copyright © 1926 (Renewed 1953)
All rights for the extended term administered by Fred Ahlert Music Corporation on behalf of Olde Clover Leaf Music
All rights for the extended term administered by Ray Henderson Music on behalf of Ray Henderson

Copyright © 1942 (Renewed 1969) by Famous Music Corporation in the U.S.A.
Rights for the world outside the U.S.A. Controlled by EMI Robbins Catalog Inc. (Publishing)
and Warner Bros. Publications U.S. Inc. (Print)

Copyright © 1944 by Bourne Co. and Universal - PolyGram International Publishing, Inc. in the United States
Copyright Renewed
Rights for the world outside the United States Controlled by EMI Feist Catalog Inc. (Publishing)
and Warner Bros. Publications U.S. Inc. (Print)

Copyright © 1964 (Renewed) by Hancock Music (BMI)

Copyright © 1937 (Renewed 1965) and Assigned to Famous Music Corporation and EMI Mills Music Inc. in the U.S.A.
Rights for the world outside the U.S.A. Controlled by EMI Mills Music Inc. (Publishing)
and Warner Bros. Publications U.S. Inc. (Print)

Copyright © 1961 by Atzal Music, Inc.
Copyright Renewed
All Rights Administered by Unichappell Music Inc.

Copyright © 1973 (Renewed) by Hancock Music (BMI)

Copyright © 1953, 1959 (Renewed 1981, 1987) by Vogue Records Editions Musicales
Subpublisher - Criterion Music Corp.

(FAST BLUES)

CHASIN' THE TRANE

—JOHN COLTRANE

Copyright © 1977 JOWCOL MUSIC

Copyright © 1962 (Renewed 1990) by Second Floor Music

D-7b5 G7 | 2. C- N.C.

B C9 | Bb9

Ab9 | D-7b5 G7

C C- | D-7b5 G7 | C-

F- G-7b5 | F-/Ab G-7b5 | F-

D-7b5 | G7 | F-7 | Bb7

Eb-7 Ab7 | D-7b5 G7 | ⊕ C- N.C. (SOLO BREAK)

AFTER SOLOS, D.S. AL ⊕
PLAY PICKUPS

⊕ C- | D7b5(b9) | 1. G7

2. G7 | C-7(maj7)

Copyright © 1965 Jazz Horn Music
Copyright Renewed
All Rights Administered by Sony/ATV Music Publishing, 8 Music Square West, Nashville, TN 37203

E-7b5
A7#9
D-
D-7
D-6
Bbmaj7
Ebmaj7#11
F#7b5
B-7
E-(add9)/B
Gmaj7
Abmaj7
A-7
Fmaj7#11
A-7
Dmaj7b5

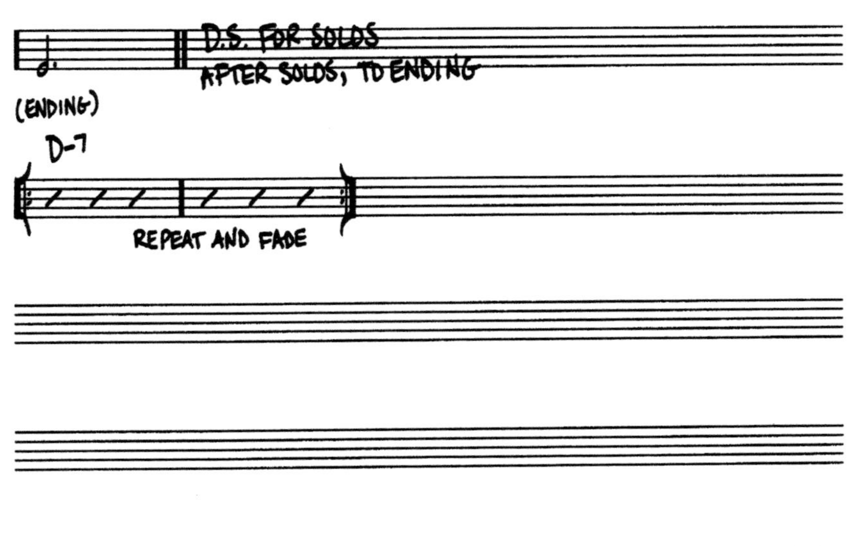
D.S. FOR SOLOS
AFTER SOLOS, TO ENDING
(ENDING)
D-7
REPEAT AND FADE

CLOSE YOUR EYES

(MED.)

-BERNICE PETKERE

G-7b5 C7b9 G-7b5 C7b9

F- G-7b5 C7b9 F- 1.

2. C-7 F7 C-7

F7 Bb7 Db7

C7b9 G-7b5 C7b9 G-7b5

C7b9 F- G-7b5 C7b9 F-

Copyright © 1932 (Renewed) BERNICE PETKERE MUSIC CO.

D♭maj7 E♭add9 F7 (FILL)

1. 2.

FINE

AFTER SOLOS, D.C. AL FINE
(TAKE REPEAT)

Copyright © 1969 (Renewed) Seventh House Ltd.

COME RAIN OR COME SHINE

(MED.)

-HAROLD ARLEN/JOHNNY MERCER

Copyright © 1946 (Renewed) by Chappell & Co. and S.A. Music Co.

Copyright © 1962 SINCERE MUSIC CO. and BENGLO MUSIC
Copyright Renewed
All Rights Administered by IRVING MUSIC, INC.

© 1967 (Renewed 1995) SCREEN GEMS-EMI MUSIC INC.

COOL BLUES

- CHARLIE PARKER

C

F7 C

D-7 G7 C

Copyright © 1961 SONGS OF UNIVERSAL, INC.
Copyright Renewed

Copyright © 1964 (Renewed 1992) by HUBTONES MUSIC CO.

COUSIN MARY

-JOHN COLTRANE

(UP)

Copyright © 1974 (Renewed 2002) JOWCOL MUSIC

CRAZEOLOGY

(BOP)

—BENNIE HARRIS

© 1950 (Renewed 1978) SCREEN GEMS-EMI MUSIC INC.

CREPUSCULE

– DJANGO REINHARDT/
F. BLANCHE

F6 G-7 A-7 G-7 C7 Fmaj7 G-7 A-7 C-7 F7

Bb6 Bb7 G-7 C7 F6 Db7 1. F6 G-7 C7 2. F6 Ab-7 Db7

Gb6 Ab-7 Bb-7 Ab-7 Db7 Gbmaj7 Ab-7 Bb-7 Ab-7 Db7

Gbmaj7 Eb-7 Ab-7 Db7 Gb6 D7 Gb6 G-7 C7

F6 G-7 A-7 G-7 C7 Fmaj7 G-7 A-7 C-7 F7

Bb6 Bb7 G-7 C7 F6 Db7 F6 (G-7 C7)

Copyright © 1941 (Renewed) by Publications Francis Day S.A.
All Rights in the U.S.A. and Canada Controlled by Jewel Music Publishing Co., Inc.

CRISS CROSS

(MED. SWING)

—THELONIOUS MONK

Copyright © 1962 (Renewed 1990) by Thelonious Music Corp.

© 1954 (Renewed 1982) BEECHWOOD MUSIC CORP.

© 1972 (Renewed 2000) EMI LONGITUDE MUSIC

(MED. SWING)

DAT DERE

-BOBBY TIMMONS

© 1960 (Renewed) by UPAM MUSIC CO., a division of Gopam Enterprises, Inc.

Copyright © 1945 (Renewed 1972, 1973) by Famous Music Corporation and Hanover Music Corp.

DEWEY SQUARE

(BOP)

– CHARLIE PARKER

Copyright © 1958 (Renewed 1986) Atlantic Music Corp.

DEXTER RIDES AGAIN

—DEXTER GORDON/EARL "BUD" POWELL

© 1950 (Renewed 1978) SCREEN GEMS-EMI MUSIC INC.

(BALLAD)

DIDN'T WE

-JIMMY WEBB

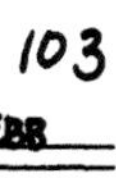

Cmaj7 A7 D-7 G7
D-7 G7 Cmaj7 B-7b5 E7b9
A- A-/G# A-/G D7/F#
Fmaj7 D-7 Bbmaj7 D-7 G7
Cmaj7 A7 D-7 G7
D-7 G7 Cmaj7 B-7b5 E7b9
A- A-/G# A-/G D7/F#
Fmaj7 C/E D-7 E-7 Fmaj7
D-7 G7 C6 (D-7 G7)

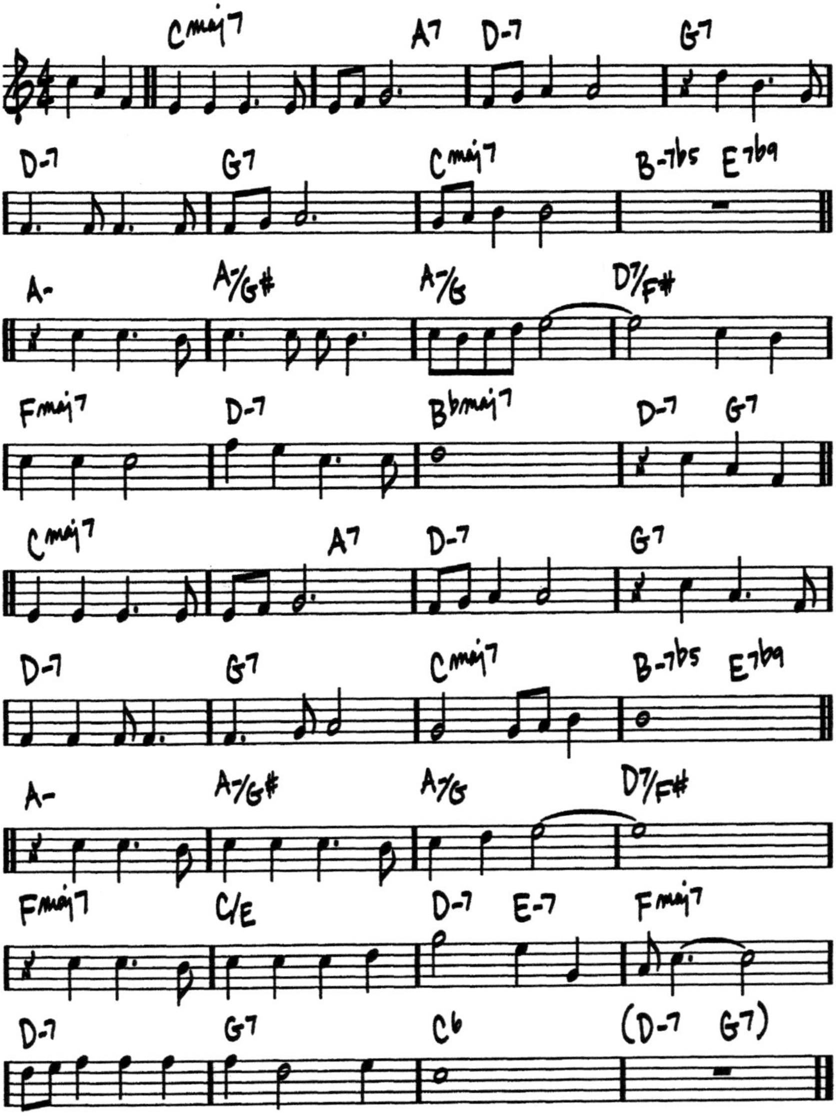

© 1966 (Renewed 1994) JOBETE MUSIC CO., INC.
All Rights Controlled and Administered by EMI APRIL MUSIC INC.

© 1925 MILLS MUSIC, INC.
© Renewed MORLEY MUSIC CO., B & G AKST PUBLISHING CO. and MILLS MUSIC, INC.

Copyright © 1965 Ipanema Music Corp.
Copyright Renewed, Assigned to Corcovado Music Corp., Ipanema Music Corp. and Luiz Oliveira

(Med.) DO I LOVE YOU BECAUSE YOU'RE BEAUTIFUL?

-RICHARD RODGERS/OSCAR HAMMERSTEIN II

Copyright © 1957 by Richard Rodgers and Oscar Hammerstein II
Copyright Renewed
WILLIAMSON MUSIC owner of publication and allied rights throughout the world

(MED. SWING)

DO NOTHIN' TILL YOU HEAR FROM ME

– DUKE ELLINGTON / BOB RUSSELL

Copyright © 1943 (Renewed 1972) by Famous Music Corporation and Harrison Music Corp. in the U.S.A.
Rights for the world outside the U.S.A. Controlled by EMI Robbins Catalog Inc. (Publishing) and Warner Bros. Publications U.S. Inc. (Print)

DO YOU KNOW WHAT IT MEANS TO MISS NEW ORLEANS

(SLOW SWING)

-EDDIE DE LANGE/LOUIS ALTER

Cmaj7 G7#5 Cmaj7 A-7 E-7 A-7 D7

D-7 D#o7 E-7 A7 1. D-7 Ab7 G7

2. D-7 G7 C6 Bb-7 Eb7 Ab6 F7

Bb-7 Eb7 Ab6 A-7 D7 Gmaj7 E-7

A-7 D7 D-7 G7 Cmaj7 G7#5 Cmaj7 A-7

E-7 A-7 D7 D-7 D#o7 E-7 A7

D7 G7 C6 (D-7 G7)

© 1946 (Renewed 1974, 2002) DE LANGE MUSIC CO. (ASCAP)/Administered by BUG MUSIC and LOUIS ALTER MUSIC PUBLICATIONS, New York
All Rights outside the United States Controlled by EDWIN H. MORRIS & COMPANY, A Division of MPL MUSIC PUBLICATIONS, INC.

DON'T EXPLAIN

Copyright © 1946 SONGS OF UNIVERSAL, INC.
Copyright Renewed

Copyright © 1941 (Renewed) by Regent Music Corporation (BMI)

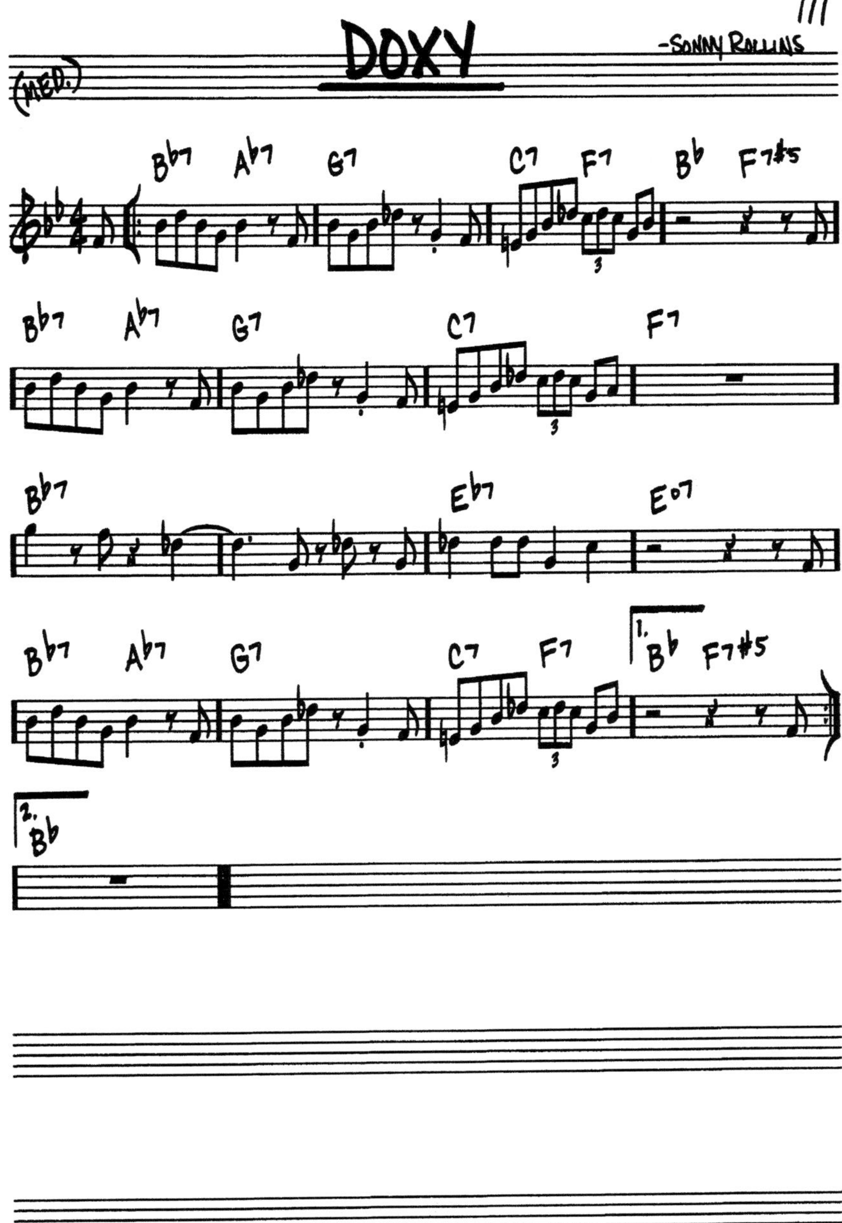

Copyright © 1963 Prestige Music
Copyright Renewed

THE DRIVE

- OLIVER E. NELSON

Copyright © 1961 (Renewed) Noslen Music Co. L.L.C.

(MED. FAST)

— HAMPTON HAWES

Bb7

Eb7 Bb7

*G-7b5/C F7#9 Bb7 1. C-7 F7

*C-7 ON SOLOS

2. (C-7 F7)

Copyright © 1956 by Fort Knox Music Inc. and Trio Music Company
Copyright Renewed

(MED. BALLAD)

EARLY AUTUMN

-RALPH BURNS/
WOODY HERMAN

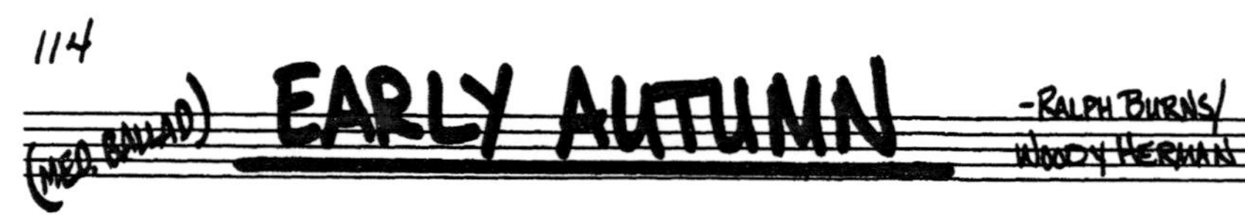

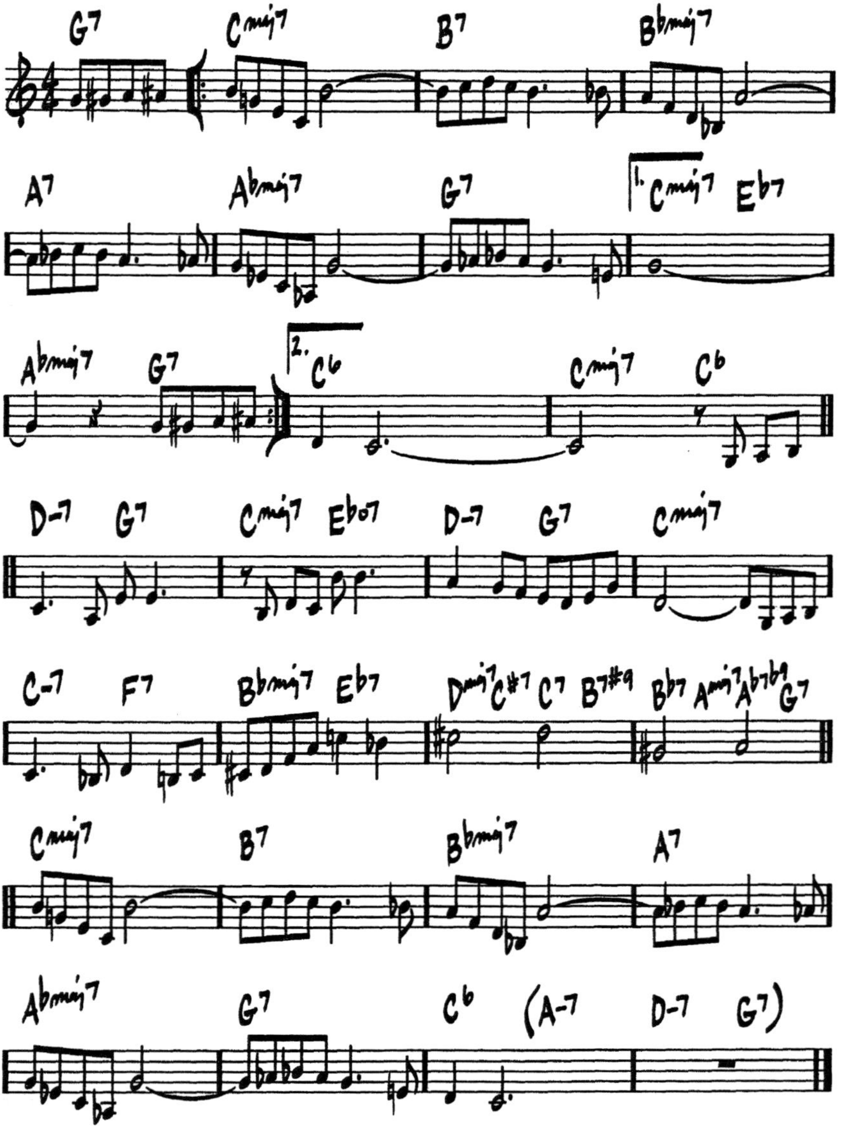

TRO - © Copyright 1949 (Renewed), 1952 (Renewed) Cromwell Music, Inc., New York, NY

Copyright © 1991 Prestige Music

Copyright © 1966 RETRAC PRODUCTIONS, INC.
Copyright Renewed

–J.J. JOHNSON

C-7 F7 B♭maj7 E♭maj7 D-7 D♭7

C-7 G7♭9 C-7 F7 1. B♭maj7 D-7♭5 D♭7

2. B♭maj7 F-7 B♭7 E♭maj7 E♭-7

B♭maj7 A-7♭5 D7♭9 G-7 C7

C-7 F7 C-7 F7

B♭maj7 E♭maj7 D-7 D♭7 C-7 G7♭9 C-7 F7

B♭maj7 (D-7♭5 D♭7)

Copyright © 1965 Prestige Music
Copyright Renewed

Copyright © 1963, 1964 by Oliver E. Nelson
Copyright Renewed
Sole Licensing and Selling Agent: Alameda Music Co.

TRO - © Copyright 1965 (Renewed) Folkways Music Publishers, Inc., New York, NY

Copyright © 1960 SANTA CECILIA CASA MUSICALE
Copyright Renewed
All Rights for United States and Canada Controlled and Administered by UNIVERSAL MUSIC CORP.

(BALLAD)

EVERYTHING I HAVE IS YOURS

-BURTON LANE/HAROLD ADAMSON

Cmaj7 Eb-7 Ab7 D-7 G7 D-7 G7#5

Cmaj7 Eb-7 Ab7 D-7 G7 B-7b5 E7b9

A- A-/G# A-/G D7/F#

E-7 A7 A-7 D7 D-7 G7

Cmaj7 Eb-7 Ab7 D-7 G7 D-7 G7#5

Cmaj7 G-7 C7 Fmaj7 B-7b5 E7b9

A- A-/G# A-/G D7/F# F-6

Cmaj7 Eb-7 Ab7 D-7 G7 C6 (D-7 G7)

Copyright © 1933 by METRO GOLDWYN MAYER, INC.
Copyright Renewed and Assigned to CHAPPELL & CO. and METRO GOLDWYN MAYER, INC.
Rights for METRO GOLDWYN MAYER, INC. Assigned to EMI CATALOGUE PARTNERSHIP
Rights for the U.S.A. Controlled and Administered by CHAPPELL & CO. and EMI ROBBINS CATALOG INC.
All Rights for the World excluding the U.S.A. Controlled and Administered by EMI ROBBINS CATALOG INC.

Copyright © 1982 by Hancock Music (BMI)

Copyright © 1983 Pat Meth Music Corp.

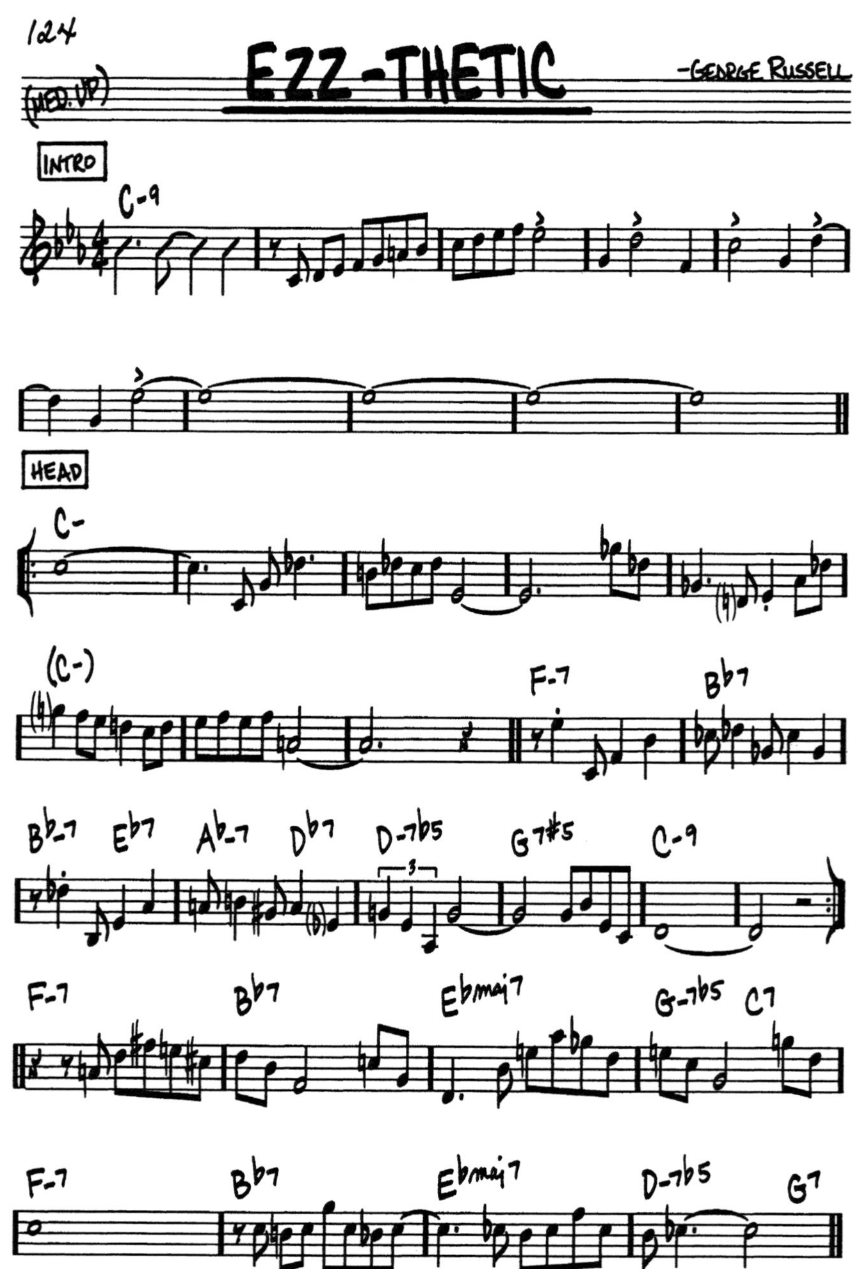

Copyright © 1949 (Renewed) RUSS-HIX MUSIC

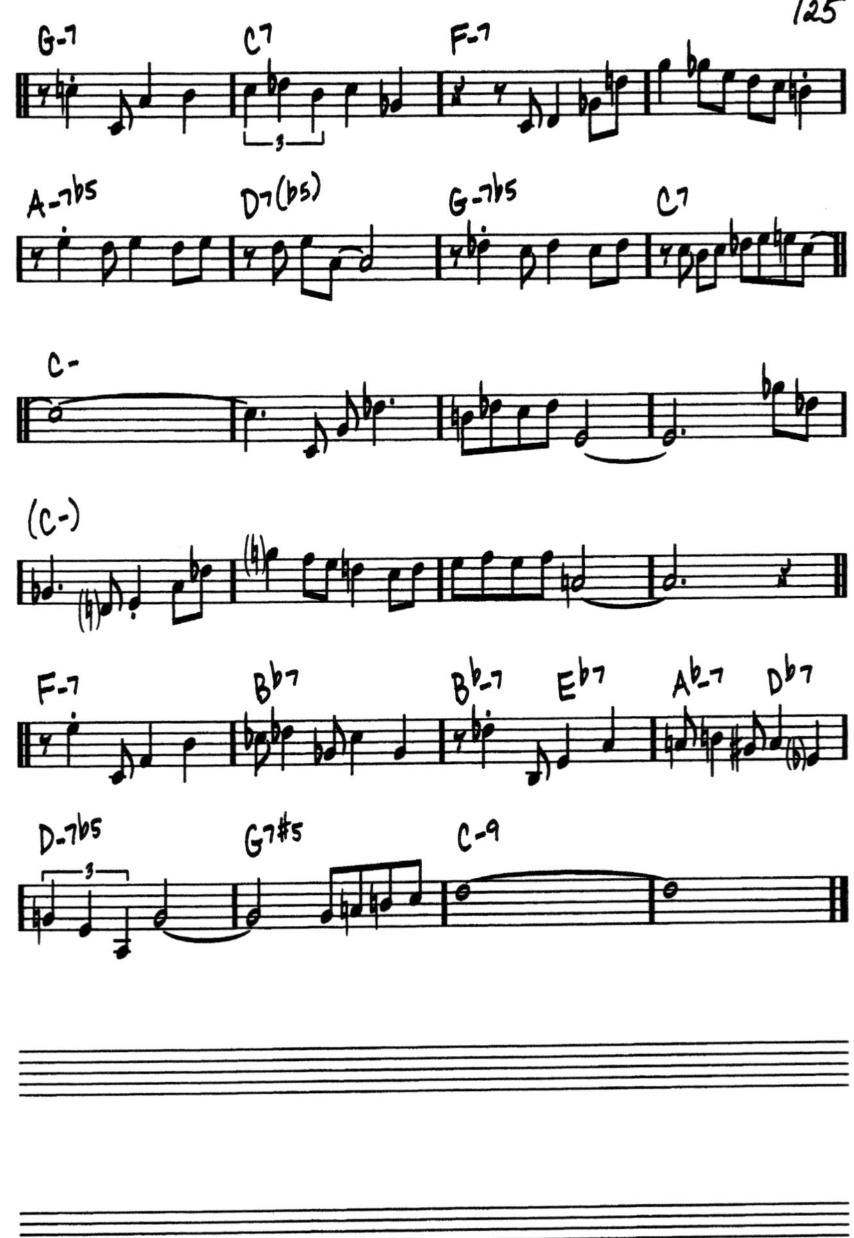
G-7
C7
F-7
A-7b5
D7(b5)
G-7b5
C7
C-
(C-)
F-7
Bb7
Bb-7
Eb7
Ab-7
Db7
D-7b5
G7#5
C-9

Copyright © 1977 by Gates Music, Inc.

(ENDING)
(D7)
G-7
C9sus4
Fmaj7
D.S. FOR SOLOS

Copyright © 1956 by Fort Knox Music Inc. and Trio Music Company
Copyright Renewed

(WP)

52nd STREET THEME

–THELONIOUS MONK

Copyright © 1944 (Renewed) by Embassy Music Corporation (BMI) and Music Sales Corporation (ASCAP)

FILTHY McNASTY

-HORACE SILVER

(MED. SWING)

INTRO

Ab7 A7 Bb7 E7 F7 Gb7

D-7b5 G7b9 C-7b5 F7sus4 Bb7#9 Ab7 A7 Bb7 ⊕ Ab7 A7 Bb7

HEAD

Bb7

Eb7 Bb7 Gb7

F7 E7 Eb7 N.C.

1.

2.

[SOLOS ON Bb BLUES]

AFTER SOLOS, LAST HEAD, D.C. (INTRO) AL ⊕

⊕ Ab7 A7 Bb7 Bb7#9

Music © 1961 by Ecaroh Music, Inc.
Copyright Renewed 1989

(MED.)

FIRST TRIP

— RON CARTER

Copyright © 1969 RETRAC PRODUCTIONS, INC.
Copyright Renewed

FIVE BROTHERS

(MED. SWING)

—GERRY MULLIGAN

⊕ A7♭9 D7 G7♭9 Cmaj7♯9(♯11)

© 1949 (Renewed 1977) BEECHWOOD MUSIC CORP.

FIVE SPOT AFTER DARK

—BENNY GOLSON

B-7

E-7 B-7

G7 F#7 B-7 (C#-7b5 F#7b9)

Copyright © 1959 (Renewed 1987) IBBOB MUSIC, INC. d/b/a TIME STEP MUSIC (ASCAP)

(BALLAD)

A FLOWER IS A LOVESOME THING

-BILLY STRAYHORN

Copyright © 1941; Renewed 1969 DreamWorks Songs (ASCAP) and Billy Strayhorn Songs, Inc. (ASCAP) for the U.S.A.
Rights for DreamWorks Songs and Billy Strayhorn Songs, Inc. Administered by Cherry Lane Music Publishing Company, Inc.

FLY ME TO THE MOON
(IN OTHER WORDS)

(MED. SWING)

-BART HOWARD

TRO - © Copyright 1954 (Renewed) Hampshire House Publishing Corp., New York, NY

Copyright © 1940 by Regent Music Corporation (BMI)
Copyright Renewed by Ragbag Music Publishing Corporation (ASCAP) and Regent Music Corporation (BMI)
All Rights for Ragbag Music Publishing Corporation Controlled and Administered by Jewel Music Publishing Co., Inc.

(BALLAD)

THE FOLKS WHO LIVE ON THE HILL

-JEROME KERN/OSCAR HAMMERSTEIN II

Cmaj7 C#o7 D-7 G7 E-7 Ebo7 D-7 G7

E-7 A-7 D-7 G7 Bb7b5 A7 D-7 G7

E-7 A7 D-7 G7 1. C6 A-7 D-7 G7

2. C6 F#-7b5 B7b9 E- F#-7b5 B7b9

E- E/D# E/D A7/C# D7 G6 G7/F E-7 A7 D-7 G7

Cmaj7 C#o7 D-7 G7 E-7 Ebo7 D-7 G7

E-7 A-7 D-7 G7 Bb7b5 A7 D-7 G7

E-7 A7 D-7 G7 E-7b5 A7 D-7 G7

C6 (A-7 D-7 G7)

Copyright © 1937 UNIVERSAL - POLYGRAM INTERNATIONAL PUBLISHING, INC.
Copyright Renewed

(MED-UP SWING)

FOUR BROTHERS

–JIMMY GIUFFRE

© 1948, 1949 (Renewed) EDWIN H. MORRIS & COMPANY, A Division of MPL Music Publishing, Inc.

FREIGHT TRANE

(MED. UP)

-TOMMY FLANAGAN

Copyright © 1969 Prestige Music
Copyright Renewed

Copyright © 1999 Prestige Music

FINE

(TO SOLOS)

SOLOS RHYTHM CHANGES

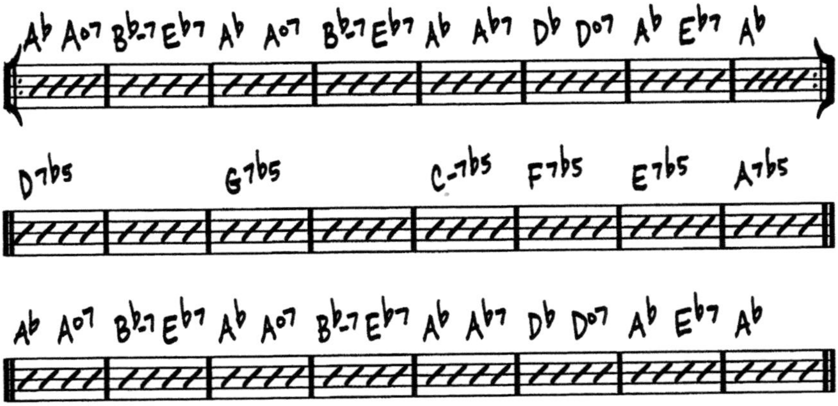

Ab A°7 Bb-7 Eb7 Ab A°7 Bb-7 Eb7 Ab Ab7 Db D°7 Ab Eb7 Ab

D7b5 G7b5 C-7b5 F7b5 E7b5 A7b5

Ab A°7 Bb-7 Eb7 Ab A°7 Bb-7 Eb7 Ab Ab7 Db D°7 Ab Eb7 Ab

AFTER SOLOS, D.C. AL FINE

Copyright © 1939 by Peer International Corporation
Copyright Renewed

THE FRIM FRAM SAUCE

(EASY SWING)

- JOE RICARDEL/
REDD EVANS

Copyright © 1946 (Renewed) by Music Sales Corporation (ASCAP)

FUNKY

– KENNY BURRELL

(MED. BLUES)

Copyright © 1965 Tru-Sound Music
Copyright Renewed

(BALLAD)

GEORGIA ON MY MIND

-HOAGY CARMICHAEL/
STUART GORRELL

Copyright © 1930 by Peermusic Ltd.
Copyright Renewed

(BRIGHT) GET ME TO THE CHURCH ON TIME

-ALAN JAY LERNER/FREDERICK LOEWE

Gmaj7 G6

Gmaj7 G6

A-7 D7 A-7 D7

A-7 D7 G6 1. 2.

Cmaj7 Gmaj7

A7 A-7 D7

Gmaj7 G6

Gmaj7 G6

Copyright © 1956 by Alan Jay Lerner and Frederick Loewe
Copyright Renewed
Chappell & Co. owner of publication and allied rights throughout the world

A-7
D7
B-7
E7
A-7
C-7
F7
B-7
E7#9
A-7
D7
B-7
E7#9
A-7
D7
G6
N.C.

GET OUT OF TOWN

(BALLAD)

–COLE PORTER

Copyright © 1938 by Chappell & Co.
Copyright Renewed, Assigned to John F. Wharton, Trustee of the Cole Porter Musical and Literary Property Trusts
Chappell & Co. owner of publication and allied rights throughout the world

Copyright © 2003 Prestige Music

THE GIFT!
(RECADO BOSSA NOVA)
(BOSSA)
-DJALMA FERREIRA/
LUIZ ANTONIO/
PAUL FRANCIS WEBSTER
FINE
© 1959, 1963 (Renewed) RYTVOC, INC. and WEBSTER MUSIC

Copyright © 1965 (Renewed 1993) by Famous Music Corporation

© 1962, 1963 (Renewed 1990, 1991) SCREEN GEMS-EMI MUSIC INC.

GREGORY IS HERE

- HORACE SILVER

(MED. LATIN)

𝄋 A

*B13(#11) *C#/B C-11

B13(#11) C-11

A-7b5 D7b9 G-7 C7

C-9 B7#9 Bbmaj7 ⊕ 1. 2.

B Eb-7 Ab7 Dbmaj7 Bb-7

Eb-7 Ab7 C-11 F7 N.C.

D.S. AL ⊕

⊕

SOLO A A B A

© 1972 by Ecaroh Music, Inc.
Copyright Renewed 2000

Copyright © 1958 (Renewed 1986) Second Floor Music

Copyright © 1978 by Thelonious Music Corp.

HALLUCINATIONS

(FAST BOP)

-EARL "BUD" POWELL

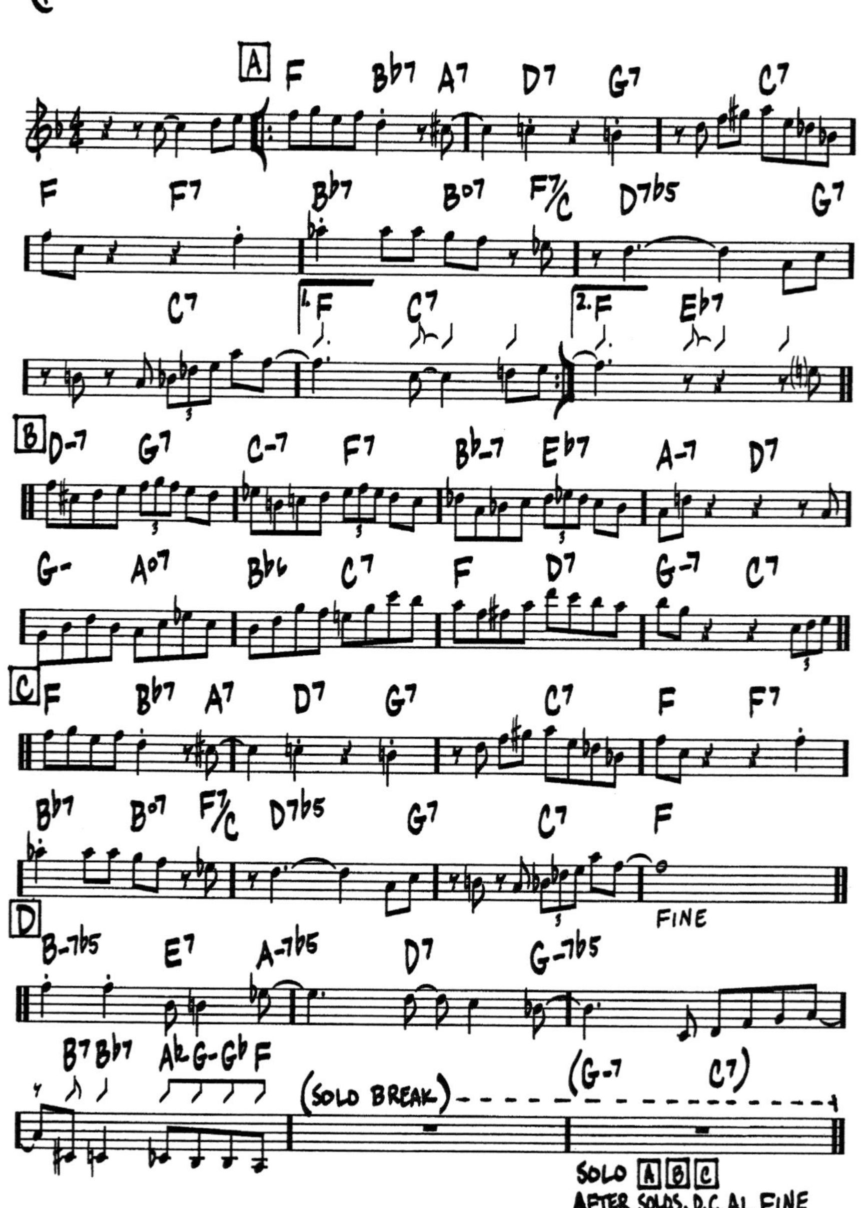

Copyright © 1965 (Renewed) by Embassy Music Corporation (BMI)

(UP)

-RUSSELL FREEMAN

Copyright © 1952 (Renewed) ENCORE MUSIC

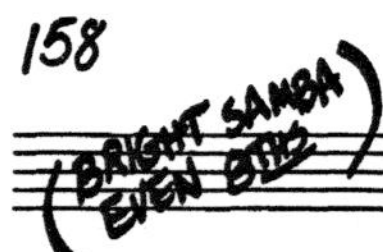

HAVONA

-JACO PASTORIUS

(BRIGHT SAMBA EVEN 8THS)

Dsus4 Csus4 Bsus4 Asus4 G#sus4 F#sus4 Bsus4 G#sus4 F#sus4 Bsus4 Esus4
(VOICE CHORDS SIM.)
F#sus4 G#sus4 Esus4
(PLAY 3x)
Bsus4
(3rd x)
F#sus4 G#sus4 Asus4 Bsus4 Esus4 Bsus4 F#sus4 G#sus4 Esus4
(TIME)
A
Emaj7(#11) Cmaj7
Bmaj7(#11) Gmaj7
3
E-7 Emaj7(#11) Cmaj7
3

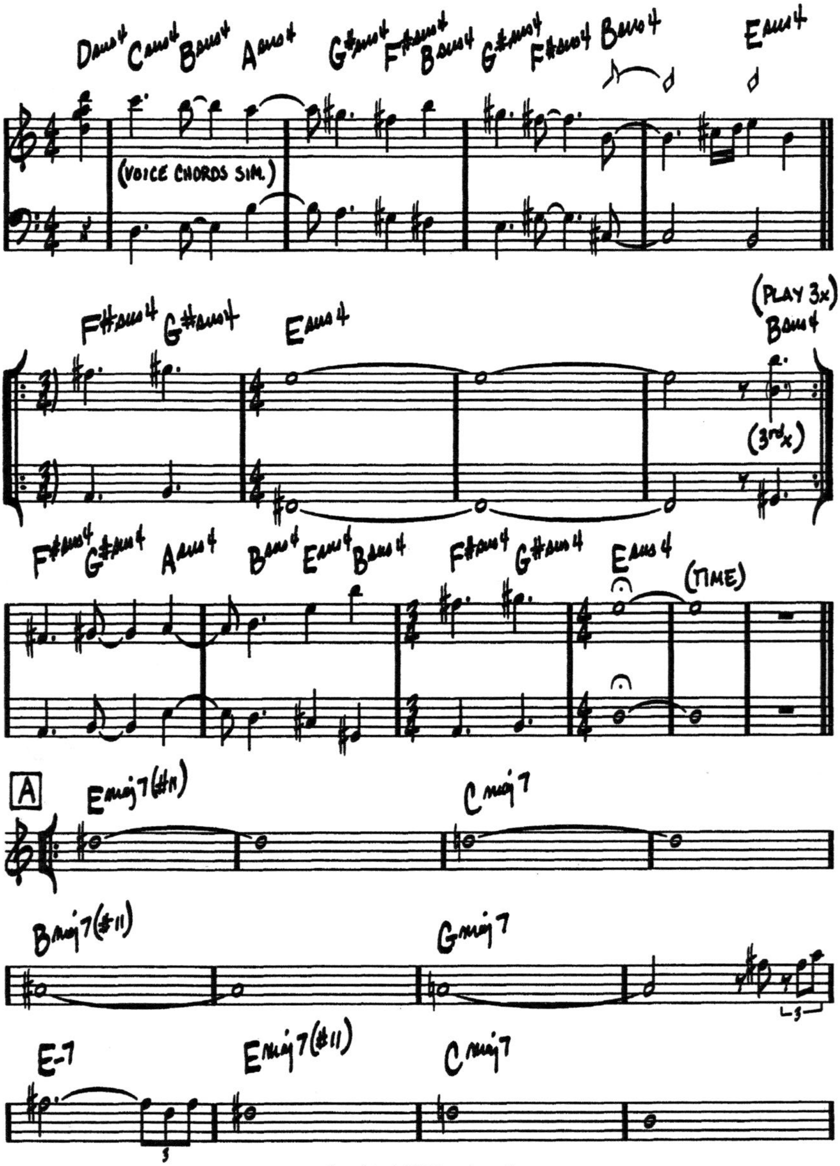

Copyright © 1976 Haapala Music
Copyright Renewed

Bmaj7(#11)
Gmaj7
Asus4 Bsus4
Asus4 Bsus4
Asus4 Bsus4
N.C.
(UNISON)
SOLO ON A
AFTER SOLOS, PLAY A TWICE
TAKE ⊕ 2nd TIME
Asus4 Bsus4
REPEAT AS DESIRED
ON CUE:
Dsus4
Csus4 Bsus4 Asus4 G#sus4 F#sus4 Bsus4 G#sus4 F#sus4 Bsus4 Esus4
F#sus4 G#sus4 Esus4

Copyright © 1967 Prestige Music
Copyright Renewed

(MED. SWING)

— RANDY WESTON

D-7 G7 Cmaj7 F7 E-7 A7

C-7 F7 1. Bb7 B7 2. D-7b5 G7b9

C-7b5 F7b9 D-7 G7b9

C-7b5 F7b9 E-7 A7 Eb-7 Ab7

D-7 G7 Cmaj7 F7 E-7 A7

C-7 F7 Bb7 B7

Copyright © 1958 (Renewed 1987) BLACK SUN MUSIC (SESAC)
All Rights Administered by MAYFLOWER MUSIC CORPORATION (ASCAP)

© 1958 William H. Bauer Inc.
Copyright Renewed

SOLOS

Cmaj7 | E-7 Ebo7 | D-7 | G7 | Cmaj7 | E-7 Ebo7 | D-7 | G7

C7 | | Fmaj7 | | D7 | | D-7 | G7

Cmaj7 | E-7 Ebo7 | D-7 | G7 | G-7 | C7 | Fmaj7 |

Fmaj7 | Bb7 | E-7 | A7 | D-7 | G7 | Cmaj7 | D-7 G7

Copyright © 1964, 1965 EDITIONS-SACHA S.A.R.L. and NORMAN GIMBEL
Copyrights Renewed
All Rights for EDITIONS-SACHA S.A.R.L. Controlled and Administered in all English speaking countries by SONGS OF UNIVERSAL, INC.
All Rights for NORMAN GIMBEL Controlled and Administered by NEW THUNDER MUSIC, INC.

Copyright © 1964 (Renewed) by Conrad Music, a division of Arc Music Corp. (BMI)

HOLY LAND

-CEDAR WALTON

Copyright © 1962 (Renewed 1990) Vernita Music

Copyright © 1929 by Chappell & Co. and Razaf Music Co. in the United States
Copyright Renewed
All Rights for Razaf Music Co. Administered by The Songwriters Guild Of America

HORACE SCOPE

– HORACE SILVER

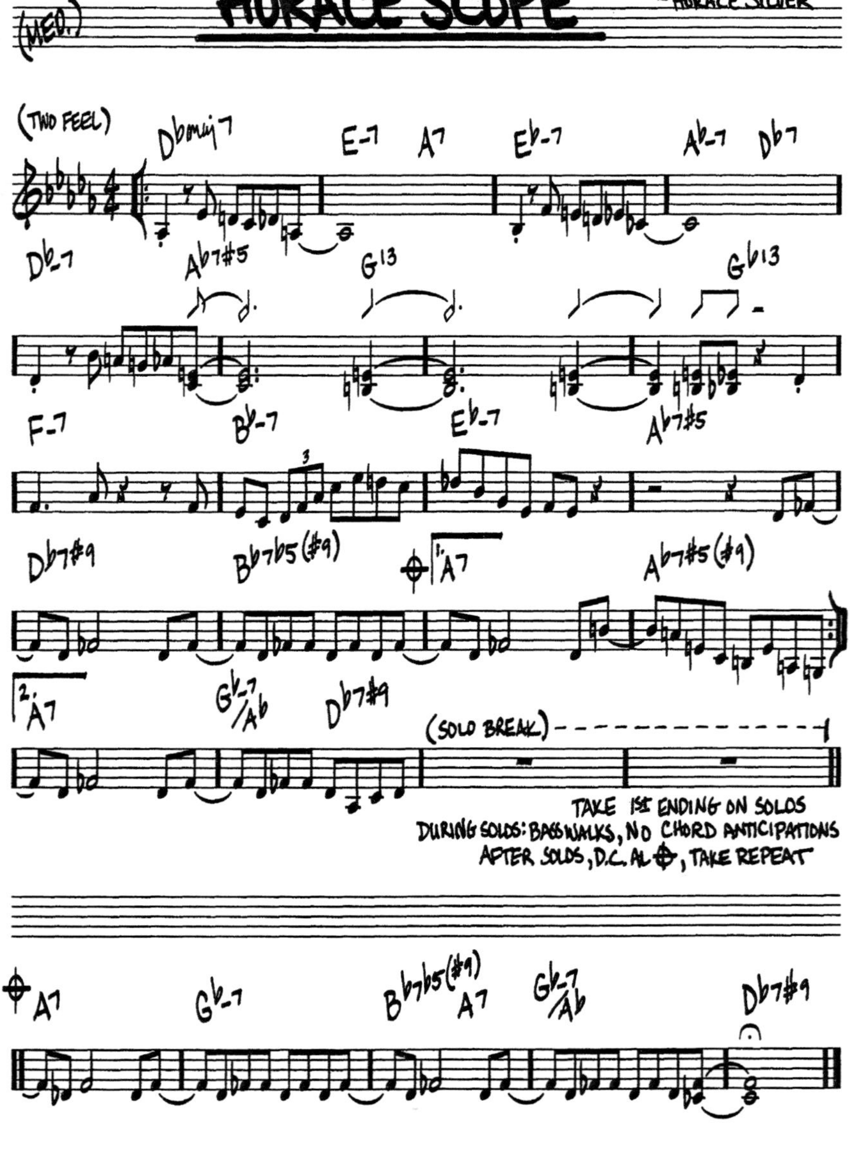

(MED.)

(TWO FEEL)

Dbmaj7 | E-7 A7 | Eb-7 | Ab-7 Db7

Db-7 Ab7#5 | G13 | | Gb13

F-7 | Bb-7 | Eb-7 | Ab7#5

Db7#9 Bb7b5(#9) | 1. A7 Ab7#5(#9)

2. A7 Gb-7/Ab Db7#9 | (SOLO BREAK)

TAKE 1ST ENDING ON SOLOS
DURING SOLOS: BASS WALKS, NO CHORD ANTICIPATIONS
AFTER SOLOS, D.C. AL ⊕, TAKE REPEAT

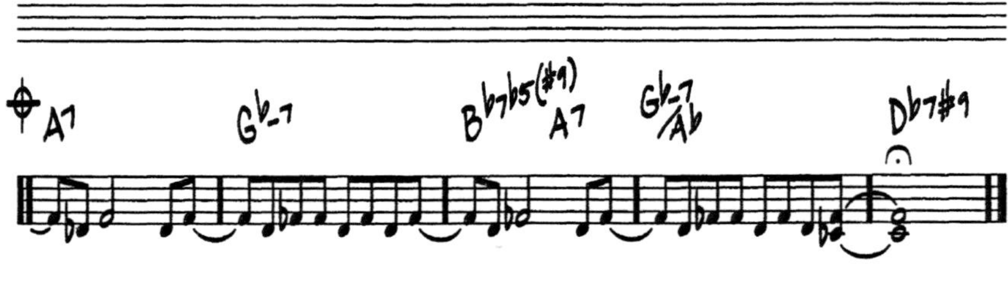

© 1956 by Ecaroh Music, Inc.
Copyright Renewed 1984

Copyright © 1948 by Bienstock Publishing Company, Jerry Leiber Music and Mike Stoller Music
Copyright Renewed

Copyright © 1969 (Renewed) by UPAM MUSIC CO., a division of Gopam Enterprises, Inc.

Copyright © 1978 UNIVERSAL MUSIC CORP.

© 1961 (Renewed) FRANK MUSIC CORP.

I DON'T STAND A GHOST OF A CHANCE

(BALLAD OR MED.)

-VICTOR YOUNG/BING CROSBY/NED WASHINGTON

Copyright © 1932 by Chappell & Co. and Mills Music, Inc.
Copyright Renewed

(MED. DR BALLAD)

I GET ALONG WITHOUT YOU VERY WELL
(EXCEPT SOMETIMES)

– HOAGY CARMICHAEL

Copyright © 1938, 1939 by Songs Of Peer, Ltd.
Copyrights Renewed

B♭maj7 E♭7
D7 A♭7
G-7
C7
C-7
F7
B♭maj7 G-7
C-7 F7
B♭maj7 E♭maj7
D-7 D♭°7
C-7
F7
C-7
F7
C-7
B7♯5
C-7
F7
B♭6 (D♭°7
C-7 F7)

Copyright © 1951 by Richard Rodgers and Oscar Hammerstein II
Copyright Renewed
WILLIAMSON MUSIC owner of publication and allied rights throughout the world

I HEAR A RHAPSODY

-GEORGE FRAGOS/ JACK BAKER/ DICK GASPARRE

Copyright © 2005 by HAL LEONARD CORPORATION

Copyright © 1967 (Renewed) Model Music Co.

I REMEMBER YOU

-VICTOR SCHERTZINGER/
JOHNNY MERCER

(MED.)

Copyright © 1942 (Renewed 1969) by Paramount Music Corporation

I THOUGHT ABOUT YOU

(MED. OR BALLAD)

-JIMMY VAN HEUSEN/ JOHNNY MERCER-

Copyright © 1939 (Renewed) by Music Sales Corporation (ASCAP) and Commander Music

D-7 G-7

C7 Fmaj7 E-7♭5 A7♭9

D-7 G-7

D-7 E-7♭5 A7♭9 D-7 1. E-7 A7♭9

2.

Copyright © 1965 UNIVERSAL - SONGS OF POLYGRAM INTERNATIONAL, INC., JONWARE MUSIC CO.,
LES PRODUCTIONS FRANCIS LEMARQUE, LES PRODUCTIONS MICHEL LEGRAND and NEW THUNDER MUSIC CO.
English Words Renewed by NORMAN GIMBEL and Assigned to GIMBEL MUSIC GROUP, INC.
(P.O. Box 15221, Beverly Hills, CA 90209 USA)

(BALLAD)

I WISH I DIDN'T LOVE YOU SO

– FRANK LOESSER

Eb6 C-7 | G-7 F-7 Bb7 | Ebmaj7 | Bb-7 Eb7 Abmaj7 Ab-7 Db7

Ebmaj7 C-7 | F-7 Bb7 | 1. Eb6 C-7 | F-7 Bb7

2. Eb6 Ab-6 | Eb6 | G-7b5 | C7

F-7 | | Db7 | C7

C-7 F7 | F-7 Bb7 | Eb6 C-7 | G-7 F-7 Bb7

Ebmaj7 Bb-7 Eb7 | Abmaj7 Ab-7 Db7 | Ebmaj7 C-7 | F-7 Bb7

Eb6 | (C-7 F-7 Bb7)

Copyright © 1947 (Renewed 1974) by Famous Music Corporation

(MED.)

I'LL KNOW

—FRANK LOESSER

© 1950 (Renewed) FRANK MUSIC CORP.

Copyright © 1951 by Barton Music Corp.
Copyright Renewed 1979 by Barton Music Corp., Sergeant Music Co. and Lehsem Music, LLC

Copyright © 1930 by Bourne Co.
Copyright Renewed

Copyright © 1945 (Renewed 1973) and Assigned to Paramount Music Corporation and Universal - PolyGram International Publishing, Inc. in the U.S.A.
Rights for the world outside the U.S.A. Controlled by Paramount Music Corporation

I'M PUTTING ALL MY EGGS IN ONE BASKET

(MED.)

-IRVING BERLIN

© Copyright 1936 by Irving Berlin
Copyright Renewed

I'VE FOUND A NEW BABY

(I FOUND A NEW BABY)

(MED.)

- JACK PALMER/
SPENCER WILLIAMS

C-7 Ab7 G7 C-7 C7

F7 Bb7 Eb6 1. Ab7 G7 2. (Eb6)

G7 C-7

F7 Bb7 G7

C-7 Ab7 G7 C-7 C7

F7 Bb7 Eb6 (Ab7 G7)

Copyright © 1926 UNIVERSAL MUSIC CORP.
Copyright Renewed

I'VE TOLD EV'RY LITTLE STAR

(MED.)

—JEROME KERN/OSCAR HAMMERSTEIN II

Copyright © 1932 UNIVERSAL - POLYGRAM INTERNATIONAL PUBLISHING, INC.
Copyright Renewed

ICE CREAM KONITZ

(BRIGHT) — LEE KONITZ

© 1958 William H. Bauer Inc.
Copyright Renewed

IDOL GOSSIP

-GERRY MULLIGAN

Copyright © 1977 by MULLIGAN PUBLISHING CO., INC.

(BALLAD OR MED.)

IF I LOVED YOU

-RICHARD RODGERS/
OSCAR HAMMERSTEIN II

Copyright © 1945 by WILLIAMSON MUSIC
Copyright Renewed

(MED.)

IF I SHOULD LOSE YOU

—LEO ROBIN/
RALPH RAINGER

Copyright © 1935 (Renewed 1962) by Famous Music Corporation

(MED.)

IF I WERE A BELL

-FRANK LOESSER

© 1950 (Renewed) FRANK MUSIC CORP.

IMAGINATION

(MED. BALLAD)

-JIMMY VAN HEUSEN/
JOHNNY BURKE

Ebmaj7 E°7 F-7 Bb7 Ebmaj7 Bb-7

G-7b5 C7b9 F- F-(maj7) F-7 Bb7 1. G-7 C7 F-7 Bb7

2. Ebmaj7 Bb-7 Eb7 Abmaj7 F-7 A-7 D7

G-7 C7 E-7b5 A7b9 D-7 G-7 C-7 F7

F-7 Bb7 Bb7#5 Ebmaj7 E°7 F-7 Bb7

Ebmaj7 Bb-7 G-7b5 C7b9 F- F-(maj7) F-7 Bb7

D-7 G7 G-7b5 C7b9 F-7 Ab°7 F-7 Bb7

Eb6 (F-7 Bb7)

Copyright © 1939, 1949 by Bourne Co., Marke Music Publishing Co., Inc., Limerick Music,
My Dad's Songs, Inc. and Reganesque Music
Copyright Renewed
All Rights for Marke Music Publishing Co., Inc. Administered by BMG Songs, a division of BMG Music Publishing NA, Inc.
All Rights for Limerick Music, My Dad's Songs, Inc. and Reganesque Music Administered by Spirit Two Music, Inc.

© 1976 (Renewed) MAYFLOWER MUSIC CORP.

© 1972 by Ecaroh Music, Inc.
Copyright Renewed 2000

IN THE STILL OF THE NIGHT

(Bright Swing)

—Cole Porter

Copyright © 1937 by Chappell & Co.
Copyright Renewed, Assigned to Robert H. Montgomery, Trustee of the Cole Porter Musical and Literary Property Trusts
Chappell & Co. owner of publication and allied rights throughout the world

F6
A7#5
Bb
G-7
C7
Fmaj7
F6
A7#5
Bb
G-7
C7
A-7b5
D7
G-7
Bb-7
Eb7
Fmaj7
B-7b5
E7b9
G-7
C7
F6/A
Abo7
G-7
C7
Fmaj7
(D7
G-7
C7)

(MED-UP SWING)

IN WALKED BUD

-THELONIOUS MONK

Copyright © 1948 (Renewed) by Embassy Music Corporation (BMI)

INDIANA
(BACK HOME AGAIN IN INDIANA)

(UP SWING)

-JAMES F. HANLEY / BALLARD MACDONALD

F Eb7 D7 G7

G-7 C7 F6 F7

Bb B°7 F D7

G7 G-7 C7

F Eb7 D7 G7

A7 D- Bb-7

F A7 D- D-/C B°7

A-7 D-7 G-7 C7 F6 (G-7 C7)

Copyright © 2005 by HAL LEONARD CORPORATION

Copyright © 1965 MIYAKO MUSIC
Copyright Renewed
All Rights Administered by IRVING MUSIC, INC.

Copyright © 1982 McCoy Tyner Music

(MED.)

IT COULD HAPPEN TO YOU

- JAMES VAN HEUSEN
JOHNNY BURKE

Copyright © 1944 (Renewed 1971) by Famous Music Corporation

(BALLAD)

IT MIGHT AS WELL BE SPRING

– RICHARD RODGERS / OSCAR HAMMERSTEIN II

Gmaj7 A-7/D Gmaj7 A-7/D Gmaj7 D-7 G7

Cmaj7 D/C G/B B♭7 1. A-7 D7 B-7 E7 A-7 D7

2. A-7 D7 G6 D-7 G7 C6 A-7 D-7 G7

D-7 G7 Cmaj7 B-7♭5 E7 A-7 A-7/G F♯-7♭5 B7

E-7 A7 A-7 D7 Gmaj7 A-7/D Gmaj7 A-7/D

Gmaj7 D-7 G7 Cmaj7 D/C G/B B♭7

A-7 D7 B7 E7 A7 A-7 D7

B-7 E-7 A7 B♭°7 B-7 E-7 A-7 D7

G6 (A-7 D7)

Copyright © 1945 by WILLIAMSON MUSIC
Copyright Renewed

IT WILL HAVE TO DO UNTIL THE REAL THING COMES ALONG

(BALLAD)

–MANN HOLINER/ALBERTA NICHOLS/SAUL CHAPLIN/L.E. FREEMAN/SAMMY CAHN

Ebmaj7 Bb7#5 Ebmaj7 D7#5 G-7 C7

F-7 Bb7 1. Eb6 C-7 F-7 Bb7

2. Eb6 Ab6 A-7b5 D7 Gmaj7 G#o7 A-7 D7

G6/B Bbo7 A-7 D7 Gmaj7 G#o7 A-7 D7

G6 Go7 F-7 Bb7 Ebmaj7 Bb7#5

Ebmaj7 D7#5 G-7 C7 F-7 Bb7

Eb6 Ab6 Eb6 (F-7 Bb7)

Copyright © 1936 by Chappell & Co. and Cahn Music Company
Copyright Renewed
All Rights for Cahn Music Company Administered by Cherry Lane Music Publishing Company, Inc. and DreamWorks Songs

Copyright © 1939 by Bourne Co.
Copyright Renewed

IT'S ALL RIGHT WITH ME

(MED. UP SWING)

- COLE PORTER

Copyright Renewed, Assigned to Robert H. Montgomery, Trustee of the Cole Porter Musical and Literary Property Trusts
Chappell & Co. owner of publication and allied rights throughout the world

(MED.)

IT'S ONLY A PAPER MOON

–HAROLD ARLEN/
BILLY ROSE/
E.Y. HARBURG

© 1933 (Renewed) CHAPPELL & CO., GLOCCA MORRA MUSIC and S.A. MUSIC CO.

(SLOW SWING)

IT'S SO PEACEFUL IN THE COUNTRY

-ALEC WILDER

TRO - © Copyright 1941 (Renewed) Ludlow Music, Inc., New York, NY

(BRIGHT BLUES)

JACKIE

-HAMPTON HAWES

Copyright © 1965 Prestige Music
Copyright Renewed

© 1960 (Renewed) by UPAM MUSIC CO., a division of Gopam Enterprises, Inc.

Copyright © 1961, 1968 (Renewed) by TAGGIE MUSIC CO., a division of Gopam Enterprises, Inc.

(MED.)

JITTERBUG WALTZ

-THOMAS "FATS" WALLER

Copyright © 1942 by Chappell & Co.
Copyright Renewed

(Funky Blues)

THE JODY GRIND

— Horace Silver

© 1967 by Ecaroh Music, Inc.
Copyright Renewed 1995

© 1970 (Renewed) by UPAM MUSIC CO., a division of Gopam Enterprises, Inc.

Copyright © 1956; Renewed and Assigned to LGL Music Co.
Administered by Larry Spier, Inc., New York

Copyright © 1949 (Renewed 1977) Atlantic Music Corp., Travis Music Co. and United Artists Music Co., Inc.

(MED. FAST)

JUNE IS BUSTIN' OUT ALL OVER

-RICHARD RODGERS/OSCAR HAMMERSTEIN II

Copyright © 1945 by WILLIAMSON MUSIC
Copyright Renewed

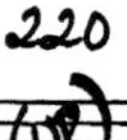

JUST A FEW

–SHORTY ROGERS

G-7 C7 | G-7 C7 | Fmaj7 G-7 | A-7 D7b9

G-7 C7 | G-7 C7 | Fmaj7 G-7 | Fmaj7

C-7 F7 | C-7 F7 | Bbmaj7 C-7 | Bbmaj7

D-7 | G7 | G-7 C7 | A-7 D7b9

G-7 C7 | G-7 C7 | Fmaj7 G-7 | Fmaj7

C-7 F7 | C-7 F7 | Bbmaj7 C-7 | Bbmaj7

Bbmaj7 | Bb-7 | A-7 | D7

F7#9 D7#9 | C7#9 C7 | F6 (SOLO BREAK ----------)

Copyright © 1954, 1955 MICHELE PUBLISHING COMPANY
Copyright Renewed
All Rights Controlled and Administered by SONGS OF UNIVERSAL, INC.

JUST A SETTIN' AND A ROCKIN'

(MED.)

-DUKE ELLINGTON/ BILLY STRAYHORN

Ab Ab/C Db Bb-7 Ab6 Db Ab/C Bb-7 Eb7 Ab6

Db Ab/C Bb-7 Bo7 Ab F-7 1. Bb-7 Eb7 Ab6 2. Bb-7 Eb7 Ab6

C- C-#5 C-6 C-#5 C- C-#5 D-7 G7

3 3

C C+ C6 C#o7 D-7 G7 Bb-7 Eb7

Ab Ab/C Db Bb-7 Ab6 Db Ab/C Bb-7 Eb7 Ab6

Db Ab/C Bb-7 Bo7 Ab F-7 Bb-7 Eb7 Ab6

Copyright © 1944 (Renewed 1972) by Famous Music Corporation, DreamWorks Songs and Billy Strayhorn Songs, Inc.
All Rights for DreamWorks Songs and Billy Strayhorn Songs, Inc. Administered by Cherry Lane Music Publishing Company, Inc.

Copyright © 1956 by Betty Comden, Adolph Green and Jule Styne
Copyright Renewed
Stratford Music Corporation, owner of publication and allied rights throughout the world
Chappell & Co., Administrator

KARY'S TRANCE

-LEE KONITZ

(MED. UP)

A-7 D-7 G7

B-7b5 E7 A-7 E7

A-7 D-7 G7

B-7b5 E7 A-7

G°7 G7b9 Cmaj7 Dbmaj7 Cmaj7

B7b9 E7

(E7) A-7

D7 B-7b5

E7 A-7

© 1956 William H. Bauer Inc.
Copyright Renewed

© 1977, 1978 IMPULSIVE MUSIC

D/F# B-7 E-7 G/A
D G-6/D D G/D Dsus4 D G-6/D 1. D D7 2. D G/D Dsus4
(INTRO RIFF)
TO C
TO D SOLO
C Gmaj A7 F#-7 B7
E-7 A7sus4 D D7/C
Bb C A-7 D7
G-7 C G/A
D.S. AL 2nd ENDING
D SOLO
D B-6 Gmaj7 B-7 D7 Gmaj7 G-6 D/F# A-7 D7
Gmaj7 G-6 D/F# B-7 B-7/E E9 G/A
D.S. AL
Bb C A-7 D7 G-7 A7
REPEAT AND FADE ON D

(JAZZ WALTZ)

KATRINA BALLERINA

-WOODY SHAW

© 1977 MAYFLOWER MUSIC CORP.

Copyright © 1967 Johen Music
Copyright Renewed

KIDS ARE PRETTY PEOPLE

(MED. SLOW)

- THAD JONES

D-7 A7#9 | D-7 | C-7 F7 Bb7 A7#9

D-7 G7 | Fmaj7/C A7/C# | D-7 D-7/C | B-7b5 E7#9

A7#9 | D-7 A7#9 | D-7 | C-7 F7 Bb7 A7#9

D-7 G7 | Fmaj7/C A7/C# | D-7 B-7b5 | F/C C7sus4

F6 A7 | D-7 Bbmaj7 | G-7 Ebmaj7 | C-7 F7

Bbmaj7 Eb7 | F/C | Eb/C | F/C

A7#9 | D-7 A7#9 | D-7 | C-7 F7 Bb7 A7#9

D-7 G7 | C7 F7 | Bb7 Eb7 | E-7b5 A7#9

D-7 (E-7b5 A7#9)

Copyright © 1963 D'Accord Music, Inc., c/o Publishers' Licensing Corporation, P.O. Box 5807, Englewood, New Jersey 07631
Copyright Renewed

Copyright © 1959 (Renewed 1987) IBBOB MUSIC, INC. d/b/a TIME STEP MUSIC (ASCAP)

Copyright © 1979 ISKA MUSIC
All Rights Administered by IRVING MUSIC, INC.

Copyright © 1977 Pat Meth Music Corp.

(BALLAD) LAST NIGHT WHEN WE WERE YOUNG

-HAROLD ARLEN/E.Y. HARBURG

© 1937 (Renewed) GLOCCA MORRA MUSIC and S.A. MUSIC CO.

(Med.)

THE LAST TIME I SAW PARIS

—JEROME KERN/OSCAR HAMMERSTEIN II

Copyright © 1940 UNIVERSAL - POLYGRAM INTERNATIONAL PUBLISHING, INC.
Copyright Renewed

LEILA

—JOHN L. (WES) MONTGOMERY

Copyright © 1957 (Renewed) by TAGGIE MUSIC CO., a division of Gopam Enterprises, Inc.

LENNIE'S PENNIES

- LENNIE TRISTANO

© 1958 William H. Bauer Inc.
Copyright Renewed

Copyright © 1978 by Thelonious Music Corp.

Copyright © 1933 by Bourne Co.
Copyright Renewed

Copyright © 1942, 1943 (Renewed 1969, 1970) by Paramount Music Corporation

Copyright © 1977 JOWCOL MUSIC

Copyright © 1950 Sony/ATV Tunes LLC
Copyright Renewed
All Rights Administered by Sony/ATV Music Publishing, 8 Music Square West, Nashville, TN 37203

Copyright © 1968 MIYAKO MUSIC
Copyright Renewed
All Rights Controlled and Administered by IRVING MUSIC, INC.

(♩= 216 FAST)

LITTLE CHICAGO FIRE

-FRANK FOSTER

Copyright © 1997 by Swing That Music, Inc.

Copyright © 1978 by Thelonious Music Corp.

Copyright © 1972 (Renewed 2000) by HUBTONES MUSIC CO.

LOCOMOTION

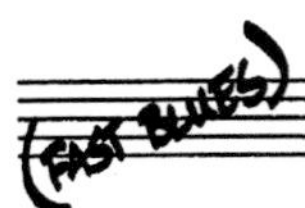

—JOHN COLTRANE

Bb7

Eb7 Bb7

C-7 F7 Bb7 1.

2. Ab7 G7

Gb7 F7

Bb7

Eb7 Bb7

C-7 F7 Bb7

Copyright © 1957 (Renewed 1985) JOWCOL MUSIC

Copyright © 1979 Pat Meth Music Corp. and Lyle Mays, Inc.

D/E E/F# G/A A/B C/D D/E F/G G/A Ab/Bb
SOLOS
Gbmaj7 Bb-7 Gbmaj7
Bb-7 Gbmaj7 F7#9 Ab Bb-
Bb-7 Gbmaj7 Bb-7 Gbmaj7
Bb-7 Gbmaj7 F7#9 Ab Bb-
Eb-7 F7b9 Gbmaj7 G-7b5
G-7/C C7 Ab-7/Db Db7 Bb-7/Eb Eb7 C-7/F F7
Bb-7 Gbmaj7 Bb-7 Gbmaj7
Bb-7 Gbmaj7 F7#9 Ab Bb-
AFTER SOLOS, D.S. AL ⊕ 2
(TAKE REPEAT AND 1ST D.S.)
⊕2
(ENDING)
Db/Eb Eb/F Gb/Ab F/G
Db/Eb Eb/F Bb/C Ab/Bb D/E E/F# G/A A/B
C/D D/E F/G
(FILL)

LONELY DREAMS

(BALLAD)

-TERRY GIBBS

Copyright © 1956 by Llee Corp.
Copyright Renewed
All Rights Administered by Melody Lane Publications, Inc.

(MED.)

LOOK FOR THE SILVER LINING

-JEROME KERN / BUDDY DESYLVA

Ebmaj7 | F-7 Bb7 | Ebmaj7 | F-7 Bb7

Ebmaj7 | Ab7 | G-7 | C-7

F-7 | Bb7 | Ebmaj7 | D-7b5 G7#9

C-7 | F7 F#o7 | G-7 C7 | F-7 Bb7

Ebmaj7 | F-7 Bb7 | Ebmaj7 | F-7 Bb7

Bb-7 | Eb7 | Abmaj7 | Ab6

F7 | F#o7 | G-7 | C7

F-7 | Bb7 | Ebmaj7 | (F-7 Bb7)

Copyright © 2005 by HAL LEONARD CORPORATION

Copyright © 1968 (Renewed) by Tempo Music, Inc. and Music Sales Corporation (ASCAP)
All Rights Administered by Music Sales Corporation

(MED.)

LOVE IS JUST AROUND THE CORNER

-LEO ROBIN/LEWIS E. GENSLER

G7 C7 Fmaj7 D7 G7 C7 Fmaj7 D7

G7 C7 A-7 D7 G7 C7 1. F6 D7 2. F6

E-7 A7 D-7 E-7 A7 D-7

G7 Go7 G7 Go7 G7 C7

G7 C7 Fmaj7 D7 G7 C7 Fmaj7 D7

G7 C7 A-7 D7 G7 C7 F6 (D7)

Copyright © 1934 (Renewed 1961) by Famous Music Corporation

Copyright © 1958 by Richard Rodgers and Oscar Hammerstein II
Copyright Renewed
WILLIAMSON MUSIC owner of publication and allied rights throughout the world

LOVE VIBRATIONS

–HORACE SILVER

(BOSSA)

D-7b5 Db7b5 | C-7 | F7

F-7 | Bb7b9 | Ebmaj7 A7b9 | Ab7 D7b9

G- | G-(#5) | G-6 | G-7 C7

F-7 | G-7 C7 | F-7 | Bb7

D-7b5 | Db7b5 | C-7 | F7 F#o7

G-7 C7b9 | F-7 Bb7 | Db6 D6 | Eb6

© 1969 by Ecaroh Music, Inc.
Copyright Renewed 1997

(Ballad)

A LOVELY WAY TO SPEND AN EVENING

–JIMMY McHUGH/HAROLD ADAMSON

Copyright © 1943 UNIVERSAL - POLYGRAM INTERNATIONAL PUBLISHING, INC.
Copyright Renewed

Copyright © 1941, 1942 UNIVERSAL MUSIC CORP.
Copyright Renewed

Copyright © 1932, 1933 (Renewed 1959, 1960) by Famous Music Corporation

Cmaj7
F#-7
B7
F-7
Bb7
E-7
A7
Eb-7
Ab7
D-7
G7
C6
(A-7
D-7
G7)

Copyright © 1960 by Betty Comden, Adolph Green and Jule Styne
Copyright Renewed
Stratford Music Corporation, owner of publication and allied rights throughout the world
Chappell & Co., Administrator

(MED. LATIN)

MANTECA

–DIZZY GILLESPIE/
WALTER GIL FULLER/
LUCIANO POZO GONZALES

Copyright © 1948 (Renewed) by Music Sales Corporation (ASCAP) and Twenty-Eighth Street Music

MEMORIES OF YOU

- EUBIE BLAKE/
ANDY RAZAF

(MED. BALLAD)

Copyright © 1930 Shapiro, Bernstein & Co., Inc., New York
Copyright Renewed; Extended term of Copyright deriving from Andy Razaf Assigned and Effective 1/1/87 to Razaf Music Co. for the USA
All Rights for Razaf Music Co. Administered by The Songwriters Guild of America

Copyright © 1963 EDIZIONI MUSICALI FORMIDABLE
Copyright Renewed
All Rights for the U.S. and Canada Controlled and Administered by UNIVERSAL MUSIC CORP.

(GOSPEL/FUNK)

MERCY, MERCY, MERCY

-JOSEF ZAWINUL

Bb Bb7/D Eb Eb/F Bb Bb7/D
Eb Eb/F Bb Bb7/D Eb Eb/F
Bb Bb7/D Eb Eb/F Bb Eb/Bb Bb7
Eb/Bb Bb Eb/Bb Bb7 Eb/Bb
Bb Bb/D Eb F Eb/F Bb Bb/D Eb
F C-7 D-7
G- F G- F G-

© 1966 (Renewed) by ZAWINUL MUSIC, a division of Gopam Enterprises, Inc.

Copyright © 1965 Prestige Music
Copyright Renewed

G7 𝄋 Cmaj7

D-7

G-7

Fmaj7 B♭maj7

B7 E7 A- A/G F#-7♭5 F7

E-7♭5 A7 D-7

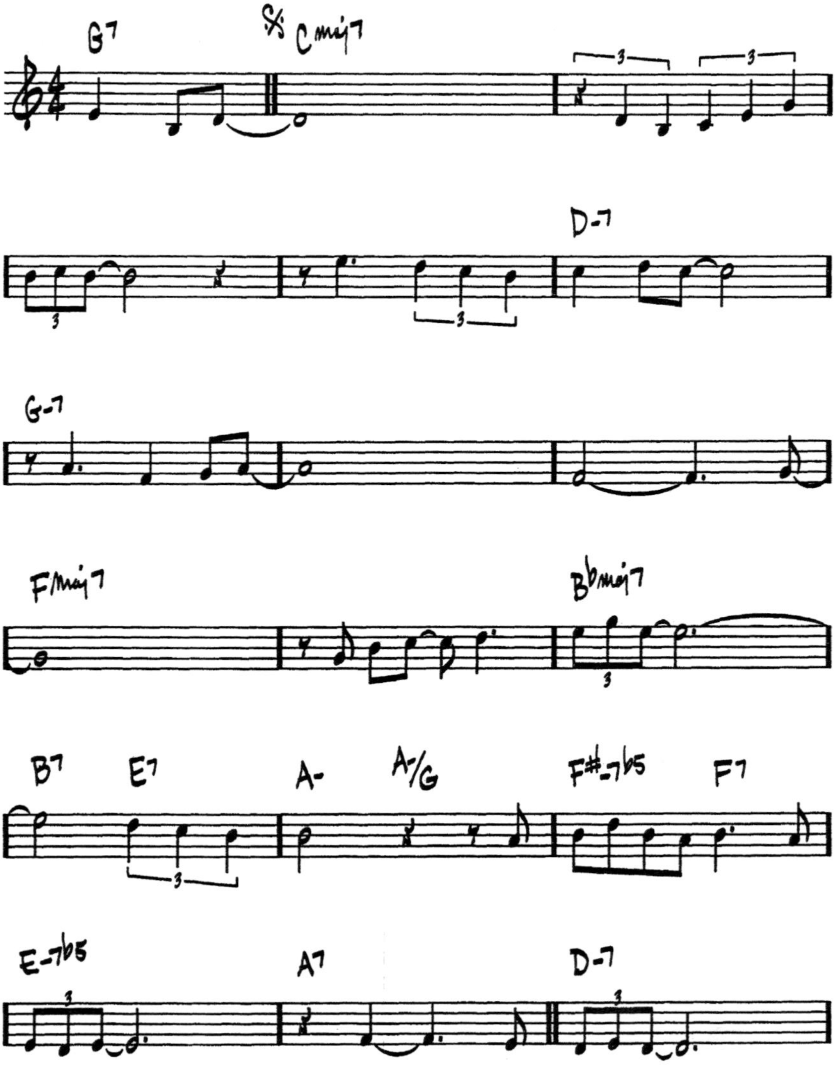

Copyright © 1958, 1966 Davis Family Publishing and Second Floor Music
Copyright Renewed
All Rights on behalf of Davis Family Publishing Administered by Sony/ATV Music Publishing,
8 Music Square West, Nashville, TN 37203
All Rights outside the U.S. Controlled by Prestige Music

Cmaj7
D-7
G-7
C7
Fmaj7
B-7b5
E7
E-7b5
A7
D-7
G7
D7
G7
D.S. FOR SOLOS
AFTER SOLOS, D.S. AL
A7
D-7
G7sus4
Bbmaj7
Db7
Cmaj7

Copyright © 1956 (Renewed 1984) Contemporary Music and Second Floor Music

(UP)

THEME FROM MR. BROADWAY

-DAVE BRUBECK

Eb7 Ab7 Eb7 Bb7

Eb7 Ab7 Eb7

Ab7 Eb-7 Ab7

Eb7 F-7 Gb6 C7

F7 E7

Eb7 C-7 F7 Bb7

REPEAT FOR SOLOS

(ENDING)

Eb7

Copyright © 1964 by Groton Music Company
Copyright Renewed
All Rights Administered by Edward B. Marks Music Company

Copyright © 1975 (Renewed) Antisia Music, Inc. (ASCAP) and Cherry Lane Music Publishing Company, Inc. (ASCAP)
Worldwide Rights for Antisia Music, Inc. Administered by Cherry Lane Music Publishing Company, Inc.

(BALLAD)

MONK'S MOOD

-THELONIOUS MONK

Copyright © 1946 (Renewed) by Embassy Music Corporation (BMI) and Music Sales Corporation (ASCAP)

Copyright © 1958 (Renewed 1986) Second Floor Music

Bb/F F
D
SOLOS
F-6 Ab7 G7#5(b9) C7#5(#9)
2
2
2
Bb-7 Ab7 G7b9 C7#5(#9) F-6 F7 F7#5(b9)
Bb-7 Ab7 G7b9 G-7b5 C7#5
F-6 Ab7 G7#5(b9) C7#5(#9)
2
2
F-6
AFTER SOLOS, D.S. AL ⊕
TAKE REPEAT
Bb/F F
E
Bb-7 Ab7 G7b9 C7#5(#9)
Bb/F F- B9(#11) Bb-7 Ab7 G7b9 C7#5(#9) F- Db/E
Ebb6(9) D7b5(#9) Dbmaj7 C7#5(#9) Bb/F F-

Copyright © 1959 (Renewed) by TAGGIE MUSIC CO., a division of Gopam Enterprises, Inc.

© 1975 by Ecaroh Music, Inc.
Copyright Renewed 2003

(BALLAD)

MOON RIVER

– HENRY MANCINI/
JOHNNY MERCER

Copyright © 1961 (Renewed 1989) by Famous Music Corporation

MOONGLOW

-WILL HUDSON/
EDDIE DE LANGE/
IRVING MILLS

Cmaj7 F7#11 G6 A7
A-7 D7 G6 Eb7 A-7 Eb7 G6
G7 / / F#7 F7 E7
A7 D7 / / Eb7 D7
Cmaj7 F7#11 G6 A7
A-7 D7 G6 Eb7 A-7 Eb7 G6

Copyright © 1934 Mills Music, Inc., New York
Copyright Renewed, Assigned to Mills Music, Inc. and Scarsdale Music Corporation, New York for the United States
All Rights outside the United States Controlled by Mills Music, Inc.

Copyright © 1946 (Renewed 1974) Atlantic Music Corp.

MORE THAN YOU KNOW

– VINCENT YOUMANS/
WILLIAM ROSE/
EDWARD ELISCU

(BALLAD)

Copyright © 1929 by Chappell & Co., WB Music Corp. and LSQ Music
Copyright Renewed
All Rights for LSQ Music Administered by The Songwriters Guild Of America

© 1979 Harlem Music, Inc. and Crosseyed Bear Music (BMI)
Administered by Harlem Music, Inc., 1762 Main Street, Buffalo, NY 14208

Copyright © 1947 Sony/ATV Tunes LLC and Peer International Corp.
Copyright Renewed
All Rights on behalf of Sony/ATV Tunes LLC Administered by Sony/ATV Music Publishing, 8 Music Square West, Nashville, TN 37203

MOVE

– Denzil De Costa Best

(UP)

© 1947 (Renewed 1975) BEECHWOOD MUSIC CORP.

MY ATTORNEY BERNIE

(MED. SAMBA)

-DAVE FRISHBERG

D-7b5 D-7b5/G D-7b5 D-7b5/G D-7b5 D-7b5/G D-7b5 D-7b5/G

D-7b5 D-7b5/G D-7b5 D-7b5/G C#o7 N.C. F-7

Bb7 Eb-7 Ab7 Dbmaj7

Gbmaj7 1. C-7 F7b9 A-7 D7 G7

2. C-7 F7b9 Ab7(#11) G7 N.C.

F9sus4 Bbmaj7 N.C. D9sus4 Gmaj7 N.C. F9sus4 Bbmaj7

N.C. D9sus4 D7#5 G- F-9 Bb13

(FILL)

Eb D7#9 G- F-9 Bb13 Eb D7#9 Gadd9 N.C.

AFTER SOLOS, D.S. AL ⊕

⊕ Eb D7b9 N.C. G-6

© 1983 Swiftwater Music
This arrangement © 2005 Swiftwater Music

MY LITTLE SUEDE SHOES

(MED. LATIN)

—CHARLIE PARKER

F-7 Bb7 Eb6 C-7 F-7 Bb7 Eb6 C-7

F-7 Bb7 G-7 C7 F-7 Bb7 1. Eb6

2. Eb6 Ab6 G-7 C7 F-7 Bb7 Eb6

Ab6 G-7 C7 F-7 Bb7 Eb6

F-7 Bb7 Eb6 C-7 F-7 Bb7 Eb6 C-7

F-7 Bb7 G-7 C7 F-7 Bb7 Eb6

Copyright © 1956 (Renewed 1984) Atlantic Music Corp.

MY OLD FLAME

-ARTHUR JOHNSTON/
SAM COSLOW

(BALLAD)

Copyright © 1934 (Renewed 1961) by Famous Music Corporation

NATURE BOY

(BALLAD EVEN 8THS)

—EDEN AHBEZ

Copyright © 1948 by Eden Ahbez
Copyright Renewed 1975 by Golden World

(BALLAD)

THE NEARNESS OF YOU

– HOAGY CARMICHAEL/
NED WASHINGTON

Copyright © 1937, 1940 (Renewed 1964, 1967) by Famous Music Corporation

© 1964 (Renewed) Charles Strouse
Worldwide publishing by Charles Strouse Music, Helene Blue Musique Ltd. administrator, www.CharlesStrouse.com

G-7 C7
(LATIN)
Fmaj7 F6 Fmaj7 F6
Fmaj7 F6 C-7 F7
(SWING)
Bbmaj7 Bb-6 A-7 D7#9
G-7 C7 F6 (G-7 C7)

Copyright © 1965 Prestige Music
Copyright Renewed

NO SPLICE

(MED. UP)

—LEE KONITZ

G-7 A-7b5 D7b9 G-7

F-7 Bb7 Ebmaj7

A-7b5 D7b9 Eb7 D7b9

G-7 Eb7 Bb-7 Eb7 Abmaj7

A-7b5 D7 G-7 A-7b5 D7b9 G-7

F-7 Bb7 Ebmaj7

E07 Bbmaj7/F

F#07 G-7 Eb7 D7b9

G-7 (A-7b5 D7b9)

© 1958 William H. Bauer Inc.
Copyright Renewed

Copyright © 1976 by MULLIGAN PUBLISHING CO., INC.
Copyright Renewed

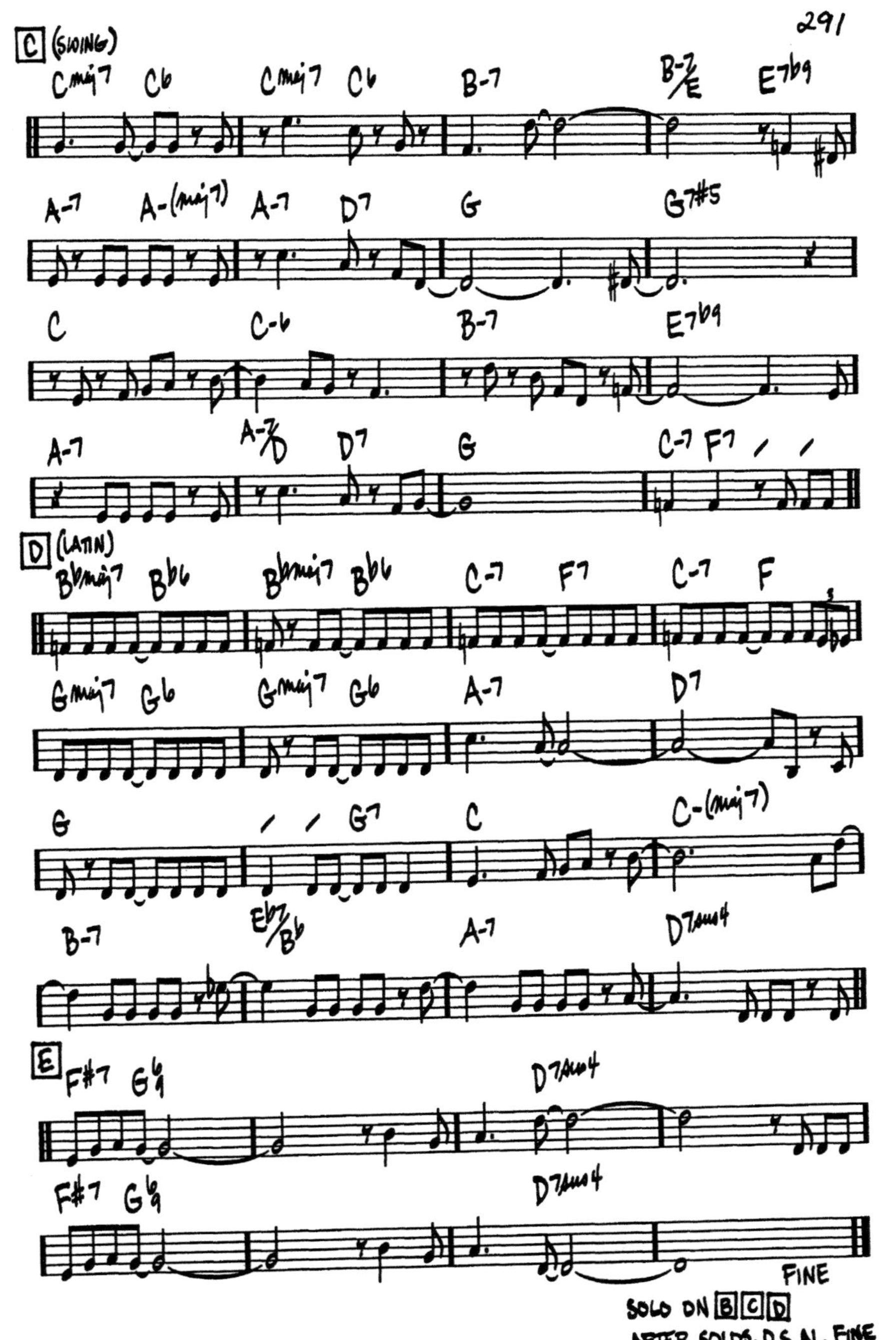
C (SWING)
Cmaj7 C6 Cmaj7 C6 B-7 B-7/E E7b9
A-7 A-(maj7) A-7 D7 G G7#5
C C-6 B-7 E7b9
A-7 A-7/D D7 G C-7 F7
D (LATIN)
Bbmaj7 Bb6 Bbmaj7 Bb6 C-7 F7 C-7 F
Gmaj7 G6 Gmaj7 G6 A-7 D7
G G7 C C-(maj7)
B-7 Eb7/Bb A-7 D7sus4
E
F#7 G6/9 D7sus4
F#7 G6/9 D7sus4
FINE
SOLO ON B C D
AFTER SOLOS, D.S. AL FINE

(MED. SLOW BLUES)

NOW SEE HOW YOU ARE

- OSCAR PETTIFORD / WOODY HARRIS

© 1956 Orpheus Music, Inc.
Copyright Renewed

NOW'S THE TIME

(FAST BLUES)

-CHARLIE PARKER

Copyright © 1945 (Renewed 1973) Atlantic Music Corp.
All Rights for the World excluding the U.S. Controlled and Administered by Screen Gems-EMI Music Inc.

© 1965 by Ecaroh Music, Inc.
Copyright Renewed 1993

OFF MINOR

(MED. SWING)

-THELONIOUS MONK

Copyright © 1947 (Renewed) by Embassy Music Corporation (BMI)

OH, WHAT A BEAUTIFUL MORNIN'

(MED. FAST WALTZ)

-RICHARD RODGERS/OSCAR HAMMERSTEIN II

Copyright © 1943 by WILLIAMSON MUSIC
Copyright Renewed

OLD DEVIL MOON

(MED.)

-BURTON LANE/
E.Y. HARBURG

Copyright © 1946 by Chappell & Co.
Copyright Renewed

(SWING) ON THE SUNNY SIDE OF THE STREET

-JIMMY McHUGH/DOROTHY FIELDS

Copyright © 1930 Shapiro, Bernstein & Co., Inc., New York and Cotton Club Publishing for the USA
Copyright Renewed
All Rights for Cotton Club Publishing Controlled and Administered by EMI April Music Inc.

Copyright © 1963 MIYAKO MUSIC
Copyright Renewed
All Rights Controlled and Administered by IRVING MUSIC, INC.

ONE FOOT IN THE GUTTER

(MED. SWING)

-CLARK TERRY

Copyright © 1958 Orpheum Music
Copyright Renewed

Copyright © 1956 by Editions Micro, Paris
Copyright © 1958 by Trafalgar Music Ltd., London for all English-speaking countries of the world
Copyright Renewed
Chappell & Co., owner of publication and allied rights for the U.S.A. and Canada

(MED. FAST)

ONE MORNING IN MAY

– HOAGY CARMICHAEL
MITCHELL PARISH

Copyright © 1933 by Songs Of Peer, Ltd. and EMI Mills Music, Inc.
Copyright Renewed
All Rights outside the USA Controlled by EMI Mills Music, Inc. (Publishing) and Warner Bros. Publications U.S. Inc. (Print)

Dmaj7 B7b9 E-7 A7

F#-7 B7b9 E-7 A7

Dmaj7 A-7 D7 Gmaj7 E-7b5 A7

D6 E-7 A7 D6 (E-7 A7)

(SLOW SWING)

OUT BACK OF THE BARN

-GERRY MULLIGAN

Copyright © 1977 by MULLIGAN PUBLISHING CO., INC.

© 1963, 1970 (Renewed 1991, 1998) EMI FULL KEEL MUSIC

Copyright © 1958 (Renewed 1986) by Thelonious Music Corp.

(UP)

PARISIAN THOROUGHFARE

-EARL "BUD" POWELL

Fmaj7 G-7 C7 A-7 D7 G-7 C7
Fmaj7 G-7 C7 Fmaj7 1. G-7 C7 2. B-7 E7
Amaj7 B-7 E7 Amaj7 A-7 D7
Gmaj7 D-7 G7 G-7 C7b5
Fmaj7 G-7 C7 A-7 D7 G-7 C7
Fmaj7 G-7 C7 Fmaj7 (G-7 C7)

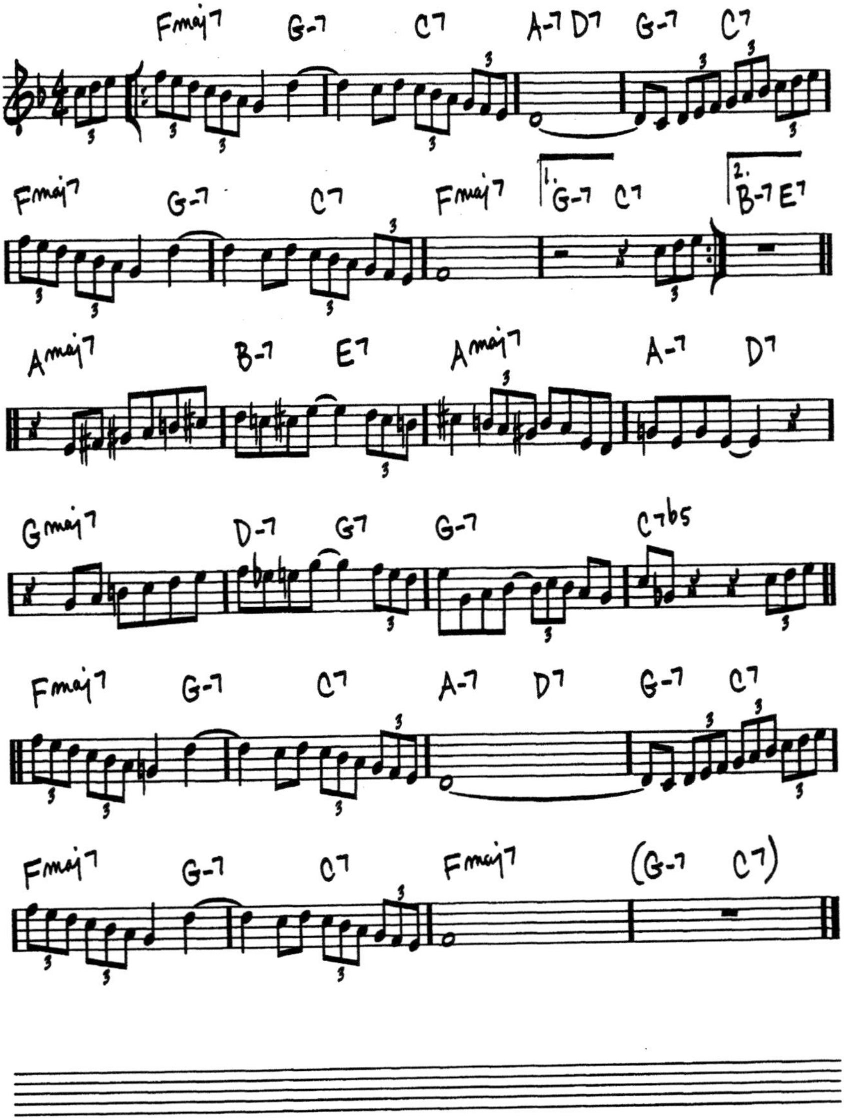

© 1953 (Renewed 1981) EMI LONGITUDE MUSIC

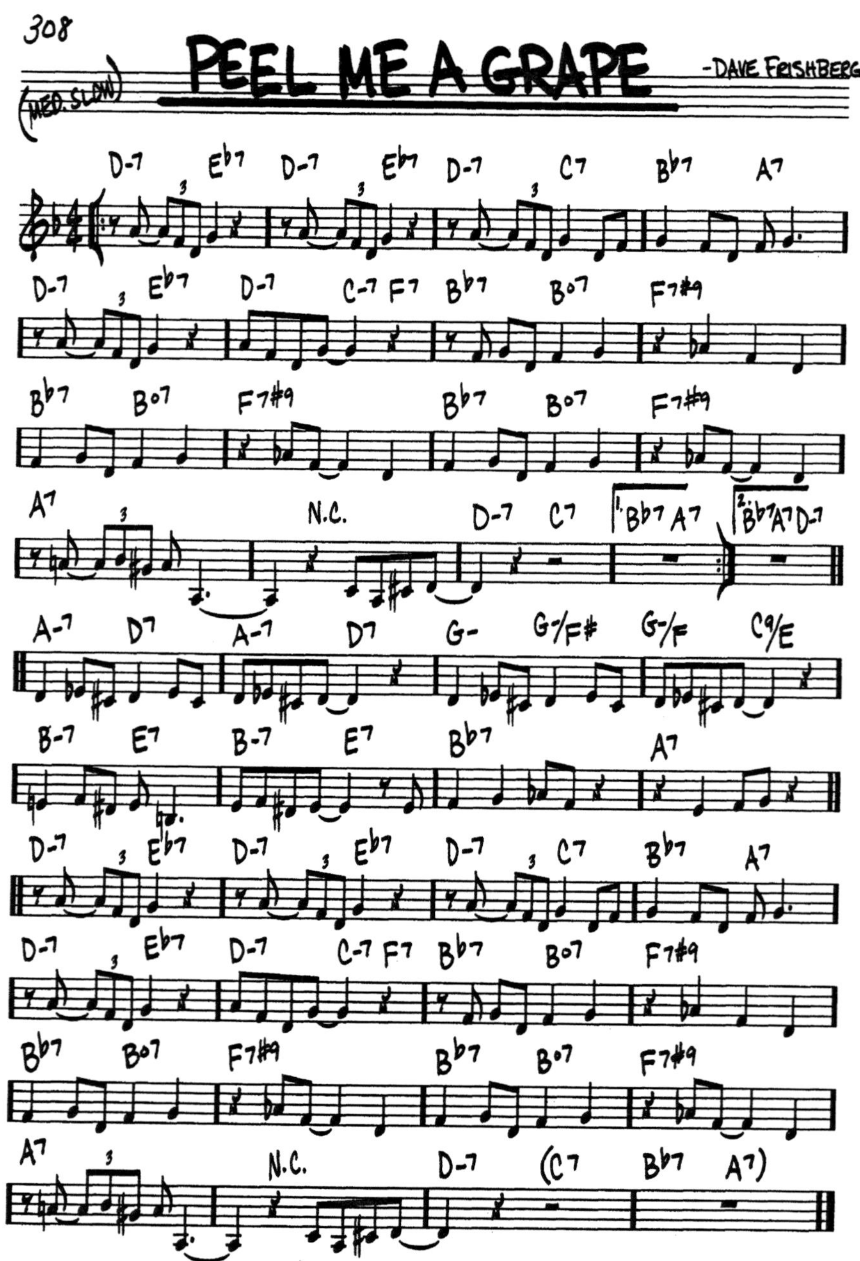

© 1962 (Renewed) Swiftwater Music

PENNIES FROM HEAVEN

–Arthur Johnston/
John Burke

(Med.)

Copyright © 1936 by Chappell & Co.
Copyright Renewed

People Will Say We're In Love

(Med. Swing)

-Richard Rodgers / Oscar Hammerstein II

Copyright © 1943 by WILLIAMSON MUSIC
Copyright Renewed

Copyright © 1942, 1944 (Renewed) by Tempo Music, Inc. and Music Sales Corporation (ASCAP)
All Rights Administered by Music Sales Corporation

Copyright © 1952 by Unichappell Music Inc.
Copyright Renewed

Copyright © 1968 Jazz Horn Music and Bopper Spock Suns Music
Copyright Renewed
All Rights on behalf of Jazz Horn Music Administered by Sony/ATV Music Publishing, 8 Music Square West, Nashville, TN 37203

Copyright © 1979 Pat Meth Music Corp. and Lyle Mays, Inc.

END HALF-TIME FEEL
Gmaj13
C
B-7
BASS PLAYS INTRO
B♭maj7
SOLO A B C
AFTER SOLOS, D.S. (PLAY PICKUPS)
VAMP INTRO TILL FADE

Copyright © 1957 by Peer International Corporation
Copyright Renewed

Copyright © 1936 UNIVERSAL - POLYGRAM INTERNATIONAL PUBLISHING, INC. and ALDI MUSIC
Copyright Renewed
All Rights for ALDI MUSIC Administered by THE SONGWRITERS GUILD OF AMERICA

(Med. Ballad)

POLKA DOTS AND MOONBEAMS

-JIMMY VAN HEUSEN/JOHNNY BURKE

Fmaj7 D-7 G-7 C7 A-7 D-7 G-7 A7

D- D-(maj7) D-7 A-7 Ab-7 1. G-7 C7 A-7 D7b9 G-7 C7

2. G-7 C7 F6 B-7b5 E7 Amaj7 A#o7 B-7 E7

C#-7 F#-7 B-7 E7 Amaj7 A#o7 B-7 E7

F#-7 B7(b9) G-7 C7 Fmaj7 D-7 G-7 C7

A-7 D-7 G-7 A7 D- D-(maj7) D-7 A-7 Ab-7

G-7 C7 F6

Copyright © 1939 by Bourne Co., Marke Music Publishing Co., Inc., Limerick Music, My Dad's Songs, Inc. and Reganesque Music
Copyright Renewed
All Rights for Marke Music Publishing Co., Inc. Administered by BMG Songs, a division of BMG Music Publishing NA, Inc.
All Rights for Limerick Music, My Dad's Songs, Inc. and Reganesque Music Administered by Spirit Two Music, Inc.

Copyright © 1948 by Chappell & Co. and J. Russell Robinson, Inc.
Copyright Renewed
All Rights for J. Russell Robinson, Inc. in the U.S. Administered by WB Music Corp.

PRISONER OF LOVE

(MED.)

–LEO ROBIN/CLARENCE GASKILL/RUSS COLUMBO

F-7 Bb7 Ebmaj7 G-7 Gb°7

F-7 D-7b5 G7 [1.] C-7 F7 F-7 Bb7 [2.] C-7 Ab-6 Eb6 D7

G-7 A-6 Bb6 C°7 G-7/D A-7 D7

G6 A-7 B-7 D7 Gmaj7 D7 Bb7

F-7 Bb7 Ebmaj7 G-7 Gb°7

F-7 D-7b5 G7 C-7 Ab-6 Eb6 (C7#9)

© 1931 (Renewed) EDWIN H. MORRIS & COMPANY, A Division of MPL Music Publishing, Inc., COLGEMS-EMI MUSIC INC. and LEO ROBIN MUSIC

PURSUANCE (PART III)

-JOHN COLTRANE

(UP)

Bb-9 Ab-9 Bb-9 Gb9 F7#9 Bb-9 Bb-9 Ab-9 Bb-9 Gb9 F7#9 Bb-9

Copyright © 1977 JOWCOL MUSIC

Copyright © 1991 Pat Meth Music Corp.

A
D-
D-(#5)
D-6
D-7
G-7
A-7
B♭maj7
C7sus4
D-
D-(#5)
D-6
C-7
F7
B7#9
B♭7♭5
A7#9
D-
G/A
SOLOS A A B A
AFTER SOLOS, D.S. AL
D-
E-/A
D-
E-/A
REPEAT AS DESIRED

(B♭)

QUICKSILVER

-Horace Silver

A♭6 G-7♭5 C7♭9

(SOLOS: D°7)

F- F- E7 E♭7

A♭6 C-7 B7 B♭-7 E♭7

1. A♭6 D♭6 D°7 A♭/E♭ F7 B♭-7 E♭7

2. A♭6 D♭6 D°7 A♭/E♭ G-7♭5 C7♭9

F- G-7♭5 C7 F- G-7♭5 C7 A♭-7 D♭7 G-7 C7

F- G-7♭5 C7 F- F-7 B♭7 B♭-7 E♭7♯9

A♭6 G-7♭5 C7♭9

F- A°7

B♭-7 C-7 B7 B♭-7 3 E♭7

A♭ D♭6 D°7 A♭/E♭ A♭6

© 1956 by Ecaroh Music, Inc.
Copyright Renewed 1984

Copyright © 1957 by Peer International Corporation
Copyright Renewed

SOLOS

Copyright © 1945 (Renewed 1973) Atlantic Music Corp.
All Rights for the World excluding the U.S. Controlled and Administered by Screen Gems - EMI Music Inc.

Copyright © 1994 Pat Meth Music Corp.

Copyright © 1958 (Renewed 1986) by Thelonious Music Corp.

(BALLAD)

RIGHT AS RAIN

-HAROLD ARLEN/
E.Y. HARBURG

© 1944 (Renewed) S.A. MUSIC CO. and GLOCCA MORRA MUSIC
All Rights for GLOCCA MORRA MUSIC Administered by NEXT DECADE MUSIC CORP.

(MED. SWING)

ROBBIN'S NEST

-SIR CHARLES THOMPSON/
"ILLINOIS" JACQUET

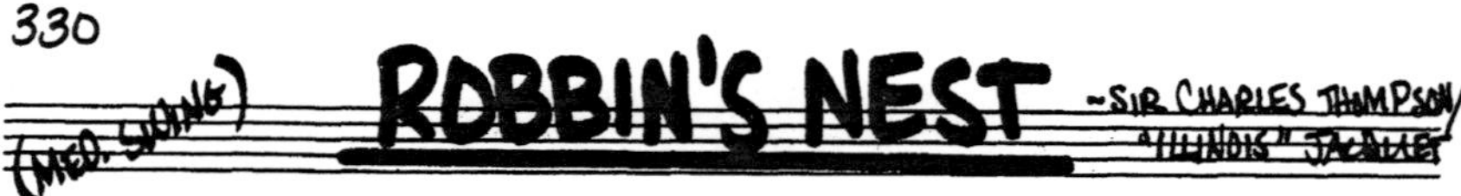

C6 Ab7
E-7 Eb°7 D-7 G7 1. C6 Eb°7
D-7 G7 2. C6 Db6 C6
E7 A7
D7 G7 D-7 G7
C6 Ab7
E-7 Eb°7 D-7 G7 C6 Db6 C6

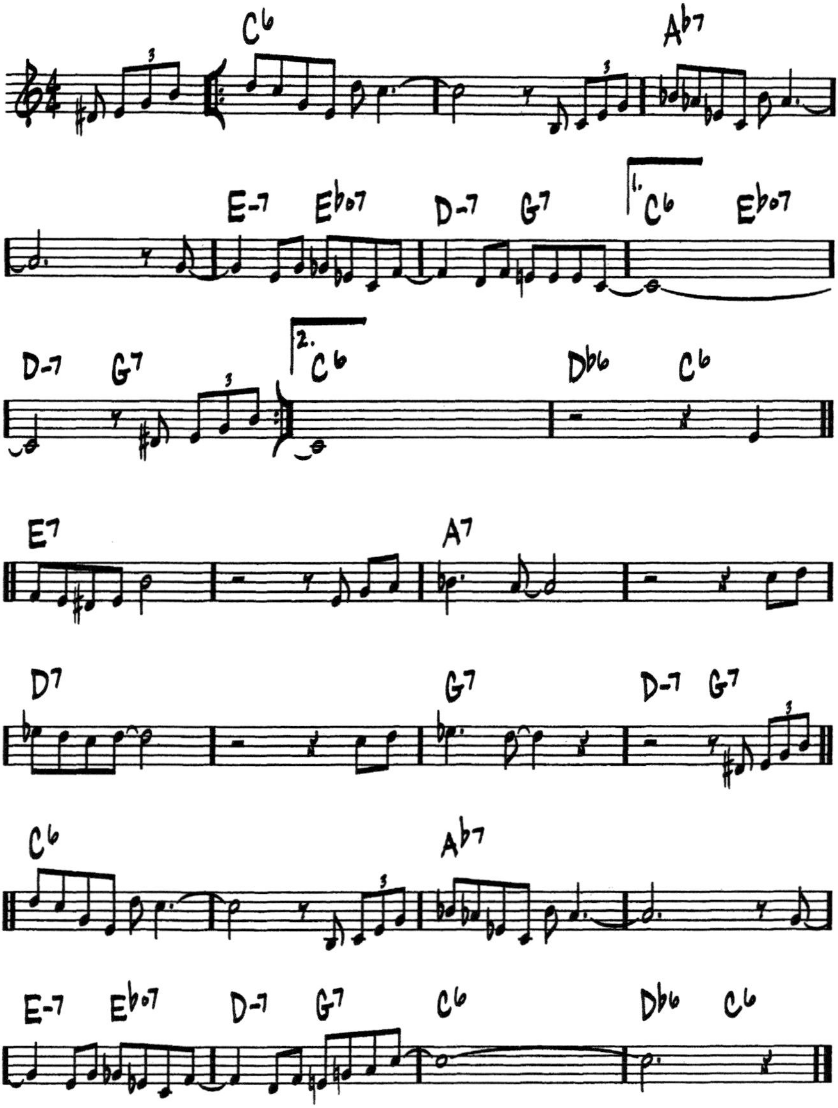

Copyright © 1947, 1948, 1951, 1952 (Renewed 1975, 1976, 1979, 1980) Atlantic Music Corp.

Copyright © 1931 (Renewed 1958) and Assigned to Famous Music Corporation and EMI Mills Music Inc. in the U.S.A.
Rights for the world outside the U.S.A. Controlled by EMI Mills Music Inc. and Warner Bros. Publications U.S. Inc.

© 1933, 1935 (Renewed) MORLEY MUSIC CO.

(MED FAST)

ROUND TRIP

-ORNETTE COLEMAN

(UNISON)

[OPEN SOLOS ON E♭]

Copyright © 1968 (Renewed) Phrase Text Music

Copyright © 1946, Renewed 1973, Assigned 1974 to Londontown Music
All Rights outside the U.S.A. controlled by E.H. Morris & Company

RUBBERNECK

– Frank Rosolino

(MED. UP)

Copyright © 1955 by Fort Knox Music Inc. and Trio Music Company
Copyright Renewed

RUSSIAN LULLABY

(MED. FAST)

-IRVING BERLIN

© Copyright 1927 by Irving Berlin
Copyright Renewed

© 1960 (Renewed), 1977 by UPAM MUSIC CO., a division of Gopam Enterprises, Inc.

SAINT JAMES INFIRMARY

(SLOW BLUES)

-JOE PRIMROSE

Copyright © 2005 by HAL LEONARD CORPORATION

ST. THOMAS

-SONNY ROLLINS

C6 E-7 A7 D-7 G7 C6

C6 E-7 A7 D-7 G7 C6

E-7b5 Bb7 A7 D-7 Ab7#5 G7

C6 C7/E F6 F#o7 C6/G G7 C6

REPEAT HEAD IN/OUT

Copyright © 1963 Prestige Music
Copyright Renewed

Copyright © 1943 UNIVERSAL MUSIC CORP.
Copyright Renewed

Copyright © 1962 (Renewed 1990) Second Floor Music

Copyright © 1940 (Renewed 1967) by Famous Music Corporation

(MED.)

SENTIMENTAL JOURNEY

- BUD GREEN/
LES BROWN/
BEN HOMER

© 1944 (Renewed) MORLEY MUSIC CO.

TRO - © Copyright 1938 (Renewed) Hampshire House Publishing Corp., New York and Chappell & Co., Los Angeles, CA

(JAZZ WALTZ)

SERENADE TO A SOUL SISTER

-HORACE SILVER

© 1968 by Ecaroh Music, Inc.
Copyright Renewed 1996

Copyright © 1962 Prestige Music
Copyright Renewed

Copyright © 1910, 1924, 1948 Shapiro, Bernstein & Co., Inc., New York
Copyright Renewed

SHUTTERBUG

(UP)

-J.J. JOHNSON

G-7

C-7

G-7

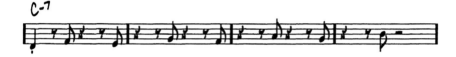

Bb-7 Eb7 A-7 D7#5(b9) G-7

Copyright © 1960 TWO JAYS PUBLISHING CO.
Copyright Renewed

© 1963 by Ecaroh Music, Inc.
Copyright Renewed 1991

SIMONE

-FRANK FOSTER

Copyright © 1971 (Renewed) by Swing That Music, Inc.

SIPPIN' AT BELLS

– MILES DAVIS

(MED. BOP)

© 1948 (Renewed 1975) SCREEN GEMS-EMI MUSIC INC.

Copyright © 1944 (Renewed 1972) Atlantic Music Corp.

Copyright © 1945 by Regent Music Corporation
Copyright Renewed by Ragbag Music Publishing Corporation (ASCAP)
All Rights for Ragbag Music Publishing Corporation Controlled and Administered by Jewel Music Publishing Co., Inc.

(BALLAD) **SMOKE GETS IN YOUR EYES**

- JEROME KERN/
OTTO HARBACH

Copyright © 1933 UNIVERSAL - POLYGRAM INTERNATIONAL PUBLISHING, INC.
Copyright Renewed

(MED.)

SOFTLY AS IN A MORNING SUNRISE

-SIGMUND ROMBERG/OSCAR HAMMERSTEIN II

Copyright © 1928 by Bambalina Music Publishing Co. and Warner Bros. Inc. in the United States
Copyright Renewed
All Rights on behalf of Bambalina Music Publishing Co. Administered by Williamson Music

Copyright © 1932 (Renewed) by Music Sales Corporation (ASCAP) and EMI Mills Music, Inc.

Fmaj7
C7#5
Fmaj7
C-7
F7
Bbmaj7
G-7b5
C7
F6
D-7
G-7
C7
Fmaj7
C7#5
Bb7
A7#5
D-7
G7
Bbmaj7
G-7b5
C7
F6
(G-7
C7)

SOME OTHER BLUES

—JOHN COLTRANE

Copyright © 1977 JOWCOL MUSIC

Copyright © 1983 Pat Meth Music Corp.

TRO - © Copyright 1978, 1983 Melody Trails, Inc., New York, NY

SOUL EYES

(BALLAD)

—MAL WALDRON

C-7 G7b9 C-7 F7

F-7 Bb7#9 G-7b5 C7b9

Abmaj7 A-7b5 D7b9 Gmaj7 Db7(#11)

Gbmaj7 F-7 Bb7 Ebmaj7 D-7b5 G7b9

C-7 G7b9 C-7 F7

F-7 Bb7#9 G-7b5 C7b9

Abmaj7 A-7b5 D7b9 G-7b5 C7b9

F-7 Bb7#9 Ebmaj7 (D-7b5 G7b9)

Copyright © 1964 Prestige Music
Copyright Renewed

© 1962 Carbaby Music
Copyright Renewed

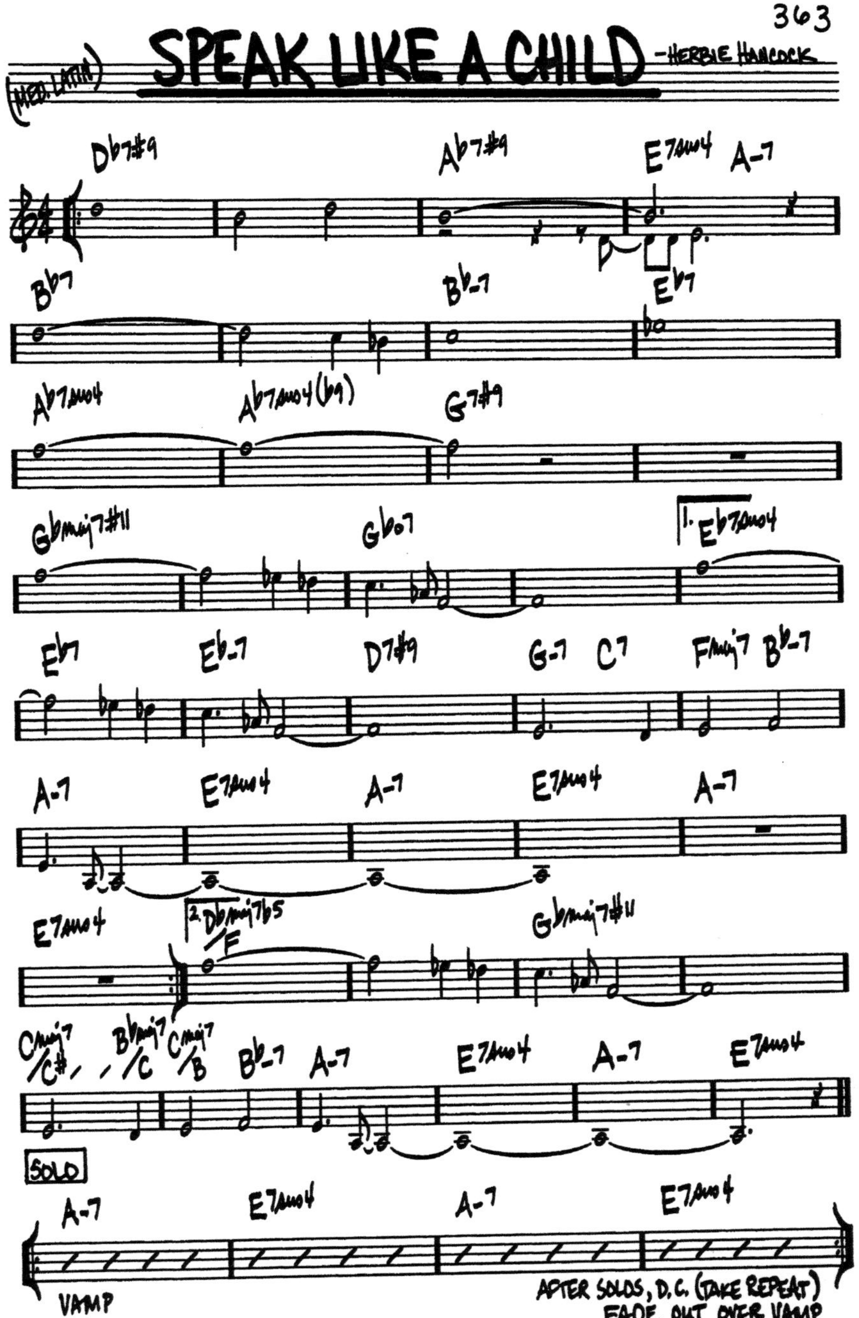

Copyright © 1982 by Hancock Music (BMI)

TRO - © Copyright 1943 (Renewed) Hampshire House Publishing Corp., New York and Chappell & Co., Los Angeles, CA

Copyright © 1977 JONCOL MUSIC

Copyright © 2005 by HAL LEONARD CORPORATION

Copyright © 1928, 1929 by Songs Of Peer, Ltd. and EMI Mills Music, Inc.
Copyrights Renewed
All Rights outside the USA Controlled by EMI Mills Music, Inc. (Publishing) and Warner Bros. Publications U.S. Inc. (Print)

STRAIGHT LIFE

-FREDDIE HUBBARD

F7 Eb7 F7 Eb7

F7 Eb7 F7 Eb7

F7 Eb7 F7 Eb7

F7 Eb7 F7 Eb7

F7 Eb7 F7 Eb7

F7 Eb7 F7 1. Eb7

2. Eb7

Copyright © 1972 (Renewed 2000) by HUBTONES MUSIC CO.

STRAYHORN 2

-Gerry Mulligan

(Ballad)

Copyright © 1977 by MULLIGAN PUBLISHING CO., INC.

Copyright © 1963 Prestige Music
Copyright Renewed

STROLLIN'

– Horace Silver

(MED.)

© 1960, 1991 by Ecaroh Music, Inc.
Copyright Renewed 1988

Copyright © 1928, 1950 UNIVERSAL MUSIC CORP.
Copyright Renewed

© 1958 William H. Bauer Inc.
Copyright Renewed

(MED.)

SUDDENLY IT'S SPRING

- JAMES VAN HEUSEN
JOHNNY BURKE

Copyright © 1943 (Renewed 1970) by Famous Music Corporation

SUMMER IN CENTRAL PARK

(JAZZ WALTZ)

- HORACE SILVER

Fmaj7 A7#5 D-7 G7

Dbmaj7 Gbmaj7 G-7 A7b9

Dmaj7 D-7

Dmaj7 D-7

Dmaj7 D-7

Dmaj7 G-7 C7b9

Fmaj7 A7#5 D-7 G7

Dbmaj7 Gbmaj7 Amaj7 Dmaj7

Dbmaj7 G-7 C7b9

Abmaj7 Gbmaj7b5 Fmaj7 G-7 C7b9

AFTER SOLOS, D.C. AL ⊕

⊕ G-7 C7b9 Abmaj7 Gbmaj7b5 Fmaj7

Copyright © 1972 by Ecaroh Music, Inc.
Copyright Renewed 2000

© 1929 EDWIN H. MORRIS & COMPANY, A Division of MPL Music Publishing, Inc.
© Renewed 1957 MORLEY MUSIC CO.

Copyright © 1928 Shapiro, Bernstein & Co., Inc., New York
Copyright Renewed

Copyright © 1962 by Richard Rodgers
Copyright Renewed
WILLIAMSON MUSIC owner of publication and allied rights throughout the world

THE SWINGIN' SHEPHERD BLUES

(MED. SLOW)

—MOE KOFFMAN/RHODA ROBERTS/KENNY JACOBSON

© 1958 (Renewed 1986) EMI LONGITUDE MUSIC

Copyright © 1977 JOWCOL MUSIC

G
B
E
F#
C#
F#
FINE
SOLOS
G
Ab7
G
Ab7
G
Ab7
G
F#7
G-
Ab
G-
Ab
G-
Ab
G-
Ab
G
Ab7
G
Ab7
G
Ab7
G
F#7
E7
D7
E7
F#7
AFTER SOLOS, D.S. AL FINE

Copyright © 1939 (Renewed) by Embassy Music Corporation (BMI) in the United States
All Rights outside the United States Controlled and Administered by Universal Music Corp.

(UP)

TAKE THE COLTRANE

–DUKE ELLINGTON

Copyright © 1965 (Renewed 1993) by Famous Music Corporation in the U.S.A.
Rights for the world outside the U.S.A. Controlled by Tempo Music, Inc. c/o Music Sales Corporation

© 1971 (Renewed 1999) DIZLO MUSIC CORP.
All Rights Controlled and Administered by EMI APRIL MUSIC INC.

A♭6
F7♯5
B♭-7
E♭7
A♭6
A-7
D7
G6
E7♯5
A-7
D7
G7
C7
D.S. AL ⊕ (HEAD IN/OUT)
⊕
C7sus4
N.C.
FINE
SOLO A A B A (NO ⊕)
AFTER SOLOS, D.S. AL ⊕
(PLAY PICKUP, TAKE REPEATS)

Copyright © 1942 (Renewed 1969) by Famous Music Corporation

TEENIE'S BLUES

(MED. SWING)

- OLIVER E. NELSON

Copyright © 1961 (Renewed) Noslen Music Co. L.L.C.

Copyright © 1949 (Renewed) by Embassy Music Corporation (BMI)

TENDERLY

- WALTER GROSS / JACK LAWRENCE

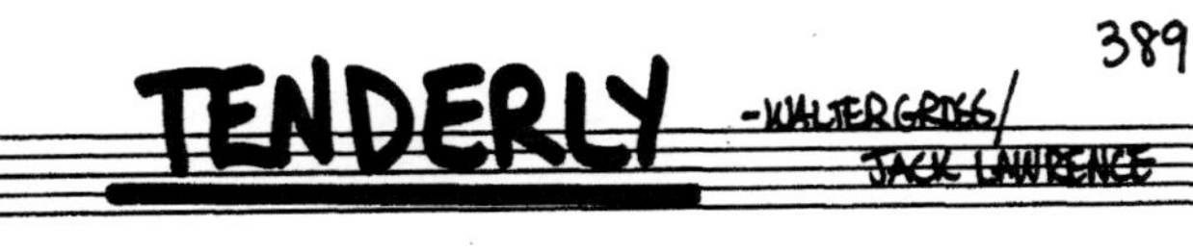

(MED. BALLAD)

Ebmaj7 Ab7(#11) Eb-7 Ab7
F-7 Db7(#11) Ebmaj7 G-7 F-7 Ebmaj7
F-7b5 Bb7 F-7b5 D-7b5 G7#5
C-7 F7 F-7 Bb7
Ebmaj7 Ab7(#11) Eb-7 Ab7
F-7 Db7(#11) Ebmaj7 G-7 F-7 Ebmaj7
F-7b5 Bb7 C-7 C-7/Bb A-7b5 D7b9
G-7 C7#5 F-7 Bb7b9 Eb6 (F-7 Bb7)

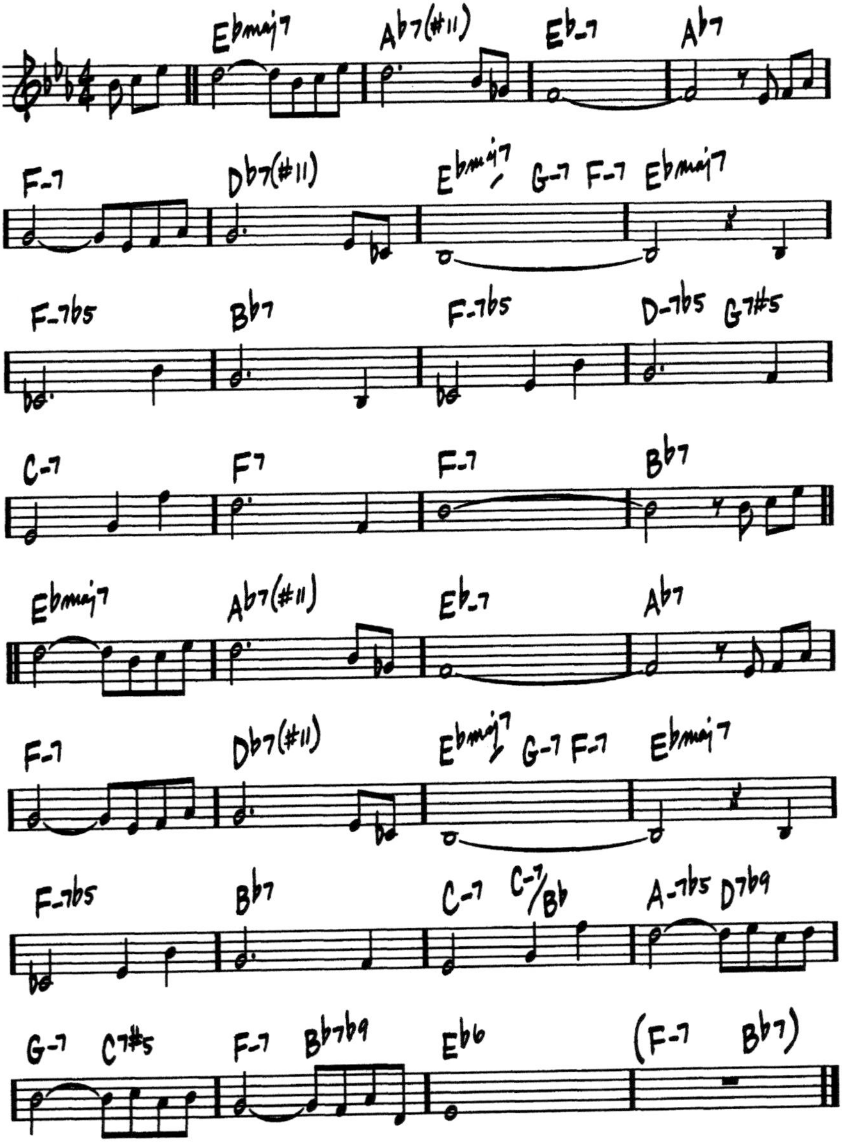

© 1946, 1947 EDWIN H. MORRIS & COMPANY, A Division of MPL Music Publishing, Inc.
Copyright Renewed, extended term of Copyright deriving from Jack Lawrence assigned and effective August 7, 2002 to RANGE ROAD MUSIC INC.

(MED. UP)

TENOR MADNESS

—SONNY ROLLINS

Copyright © 1956, 1980 Prestige Music
Copyright Renewed

Copyright © 1936 (Renewed) by Chappell & Co.
Rights for the Extended Renewal Term in the U.S. Controlled by Williamson Music and WB Music Corp. o/b/o The Estate Of Lorenz Hart

THESE FOOLISH THINGS
(REMIND ME OF YOU)

(MED. BALLAD)

- JACK STRACHEY/
HOLT MARVELL

A
Ebmaj7 C-7 F-7 Bb7 Ebmaj7 C-7

F7 Bb7 Bb-7 Eb7 Abmaj7 C7

1. F7 F-7 Bb7 2. F7 Bb7 Eb7 / A-7b5 D7

B
G- A-7b5 D7 G-7 C7 F7

Bbmaj7 G-7 C-7 F7 Bb7 Bbo7 F-7 Bb7

A
Ebmaj7 C-7 F-7 Bb7 Ebmaj7 C-7 F7 Bb7

Bb-7 Eb7 Abmaj7 C7 F7 Bb7 Eb6 (F-7 Bb7)

Copyright © 1936 by Boosey and Co. Ltd.
Copyright Renewed
All Rights for the U.S.A., Canada and Newfoundland Assigned to Bourne Co., New York

F- G°7 A♭6 G°7 F- G-7♭5 C7♭9

F- G°7 A♭6 G°7 F- C7♭9 F-

F-7 B♭7 E♭maj7

E♭-7 A♭7 D♭maj7 G-7♭5 C7♭9

F- G°7 A♭6 G°7 F- G-7♭5 C7♭9

F- G°7 A♭6 G°7 F- C7♭9 F-

Copyright © 1948 (Renewed) by Music Sales Corporation (ASCAP)

(BALLAD) THE THINGS WE DID LAST SUMMER

-JULE STYNE/SAMMY CAHN

Gmaj7 G#o7 A-7 D7 Gmaj7 B-7b5 E7b9

A-7 D7 Gmaj7 E-7 A-7 D7 1. G6 A-7 D7 2. G6

D-7 G7 D-7 G7 Cmaj7 G7 Cmaj7

E-7 A7 E-7 A7 Dmaj7 E-7 A-7 D7

Gmaj7 G#o7 A-7 D7 Gmaj7 B-7b5 E7b9

A-7 D7 B-7 E7 A-7 D7 G6 (A-7 D7)

Copyright © 1946 by Producers Music Publishing Co. and Cahn Music Company
Copyright Renewed
All Rights for Producers Music Publishing Co. Administered by Chappell & Co.
Worldwide Rights for Cahn Music Company Administered by Cherry Lane Music Publishing Company, Inc. and DreamWorks Songs

THIS I DIG OF YOU

HANK MOBLEY

Copyright © 1960 (Renewed 1988) Second Floor Music

Copyright © 1972, 1973; Renewed 2000, 2001 Songs Of The Knoll (BMI) and Embassy Music Corp. (BMI)
Worldwide Rights for Songs Of The Knoll Administered by Cherry River Music Co.

Copyright © 1974 by Kitai Music Co.
Copyright Renewed

Copyright © 1960 (Renewed 1988) by MJQ Music, Inc.

© Copyright 1937 by Irving Berlin
Copyright Renewed

TILL THERE WAS YOU

(BALLAD)

– MEREDITH WILLSON

Ebmaj7 E°7 F-7 Ab-7 Db9

Ebmaj7 G-7 Gb-7 F-7 Bb7 | 1. G-7 Gb7 F-7 Bb7

2. Eb6 Ab-6 Ebmaj7 Abmaj7 A°7

Ebmaj7 C7 F-7 G-7 A-7b5

F-7/Bb Bb7#5 Ebmaj7 E°7

F-7 Ab-7 Db9 Ebmaj7 G-7 Gb-7 F-7 Bb7

Eb6 (F-7 Bb7)

© 1950, 1957 (Renewed) FRANK MUSIC CORP. and MEREDITH WILLSON MUSIC

© 1958 by Ecaroh Music, Inc.
Copyright Renewed 1986

TOMORROW'S DESTINY

© 1976 (Renewed) MAYFLOWER MUSIC CORP.

Copyright © 1951 by Redd Evans Music
Copyright Renewed 1979 by Edward Proffitt Music and Aria Music Company
All Rights for Aria Music Company Administered by The Songwriters Guild Of America

Copyright © 1999 Prestige Music

TURNAROUND

(MED. BLUES)

- ORNETTE COLEMAN

Copyright © 1959 Composers Music
Copyright Renewed

Copyright © 1965 (Renewed 1993) Second Floor Music

(MED.)

TWO CIGARETTES IN THE DARK

-LEW POLLACK/PAUL FRANCIS WEBSTER

Copyright © 1934 (Renewed) by Webster Music Co. and Chappell & Co.
Copyright Renewed

(MED. BLUES)

TWO DEGREES EAST, THREE DEGREES WEST

—JOHN LEWIS

Copyright © 1956 (Renewed 1984) by MJQ Music, Inc.

UNTIL I MET YOU
(CORNER POCKET)

- FREDDIE GREEN
DON WOLF

(MED. SWING)

Eb-7 Ab7 Db6 F-7 Bb7

Eb-7 Ab7 Db6 1. F-7 Bb7 2. (Db6)

Ab-7 Db7 Gbmaj7

Bb-7 Eb7 Ab7 Eb-7 Ab7

Eb-7 Ab7 Db6 F-7 Bb7

Eb-7 Ab7 Db6 (F-7 Bb7)

Copyright © 1956 (Renewed 1984) EMI LONGITUDE MUSIC

WALKIN' SHOES

– GERRY MULLIGAN

(MED.)

Copyright © 1954 (Renewed 1982) Criterion Music Corp.

A WALKIN' THING

-BENNY CARTER

(MED.)

D- D-/C B-7b5 Bb7 D-/A G-7 D-/F A7/E

D- D-/C B-7b5 Bb7 D-/A G-7

1. D- E-7b5 A7b9 2. D- C-7 F7 Bb6

C-7 F7 Bb6 C-7 F7 Bb6

B-7 E7 A7 D- D-/C B-7b5 Bb7

D-/A G-7 D-/F A7/E D- D-/C

B-7b5 Bb7 D-/A G-7 D- (E-7b5 A7b9)

Copyright © 1957 Bee Cee Music Company
Copyright Renewed

Copyright © 1941 (Renewed 1969) by Famous Music Corporation in the U.S.A.
Rights for the world outside the U.S.A. Controlled by EMI Robbins Catalog Inc. and Warner Bros. Publications U.S. Inc.

(Bossa)

WATCH WHAT HAPPENS

-MICHEL LEGRAND/JACQUES DEMY/NORMAN GIMBEL

Copyright © 1964 PRODUCTIONS MICHEL LEGRAND and PRODUCTIONS FRANCIS LEMARQUE
Copyright © 1965 UNIVERSAL - SONGS OF POLYGRAM INTERNATIONAL, INC. and JONWARE MUSIC CORP.
Copyright Renewed; English words Renewed 1993 by NORMAN GIMBEL and Assigned to GIMBEL MUSIC GROUP, INC.
(P.O. Box 15221, Beverly Hills, CA 90209 USA)

Copyright © 1977 Pat Meth Music Corp.

THE WAY YOU LOOK TONIGHT

(SLOW)

-JEROME KERN / DOROTHY FIELDS

Copyright © 1936 UNIVERSAL - POLYGRAM INTERNATIONAL PUBLISHING, INC. and ALDI MUSIC
Copyright Renewed
All Rights for ALDI MUSIC Administered by THE SONGWRITERS GUILD OF AMERICA

© 1951 EDWARD KRASSNER MUSIC CO., INC.
© Renewed 1979 EDWIN H. MORRIS & COMPANY, A Division of MPL Music Publishing, Inc. and CHAPPELL & CO.

Copyright © 1947 (Renewed) by Embassy Music Corporation (BMI)
All Rights outside the United States Controlled by Music Sales Corporation (ASCAP)

© 1975 (Renewed) Desmond Music Company

© Copyright 1924 by Irving Berlin
© Arrangement Copyright 1947 by Irving Berlin
Copyright Renewed

Copyright © 1939 by Marke Music Publishing Co., Inc., Limerick Music, My Dad's Songs, Inc., Reganesque Music and Warner Bros. Inc.
Copyright Renewed
All Rights for Marke Music Publishing Co., Inc. Administered by BMG Songs, a division of BMG Music Publishing NA, Inc.
All Rights for Limerick Music, My Dad's Songs, Inc. and Reganesque Music Administered by Spirit Two Music, Inc.

(Med.)

WHEN LIGHTS ARE LOW

-BENNY CARTER/
SPENCER WILLIAMS

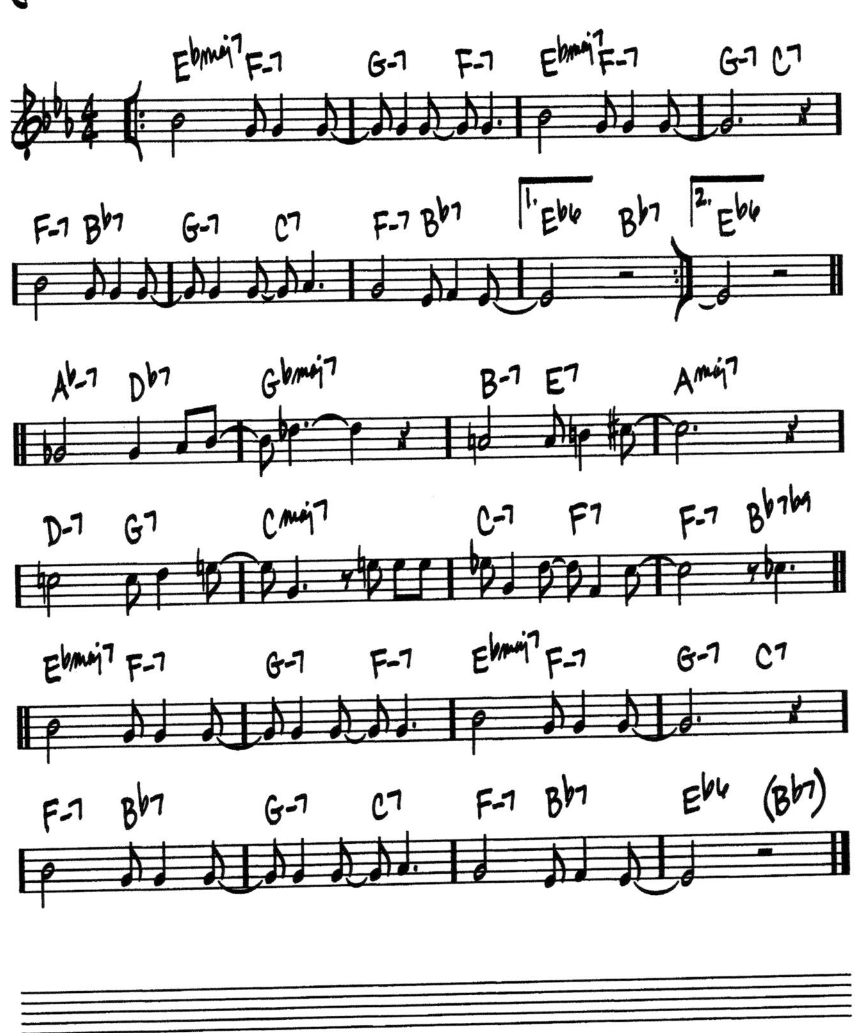

Copyright © 1936 by Bee Cee Music Company and EMI Mills Music, Inc.
Copyright Renewed

WHISPER NOT

(MED.)

-BENNY GOLSON

Copyright © 1956 (Renewed 1984) IBBOB MUSIC, INC. d/b/a TIME STEP MUSIC (ASCAP)

WHO CAN I TURN TO
(WHEN NOBODY NEEDS ME)

(MED. BALLAD)

-LESLIE BRICUSSE/ANTHONY NEWLEY

© Copyright 1964 (Renewed) Concord Music Ltd., London, England
TRO - Musical Comedy Productions, Inc., New York, controls all publication rights for the U.S.A. and Canada

Copyright © 1977 Pat Meth Music Corp.

Copyright © 1927 UNIVERSAL - POLYGRAM INTERNATIONAL PUBLISHING, INC.
Copyright Renewed

Copyright © 1932 by Bourne Co.
Copyright Renewed by Ann Ronell Music
All Rights in the U.S. Administered by The Songwriters Guild of America
All Rights outside the U.S. Administered by Bourne Co.

(MED.)

WITH A SONG IN MY HEART

- RICHARD RODGERS/ LORENZ HART

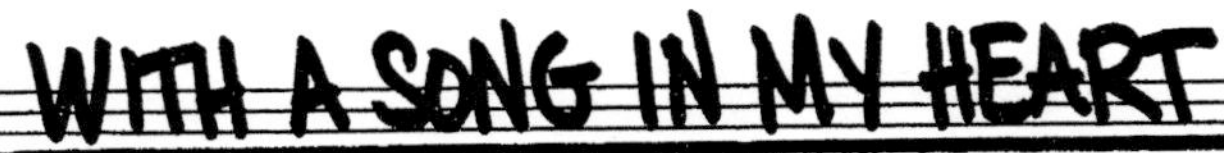

Ebmaj7 F-7 Bb7 Ebmaj7 F-7 G7b9
C-7 D-7b5 G7 C-7 D-7b5 G7b9
C-7 C-7/Bb A-7b5 1. Abmaj7 G7 C- C-/B
3
C-/Bb C-/A Abmaj7 D7 G7 C7 F-7 Bb7
3
2. Eb/Bb A-7b5 Ab-6 G-7 Gb°7 F-7 Bb7
Eb6 (F-7 Bb7)

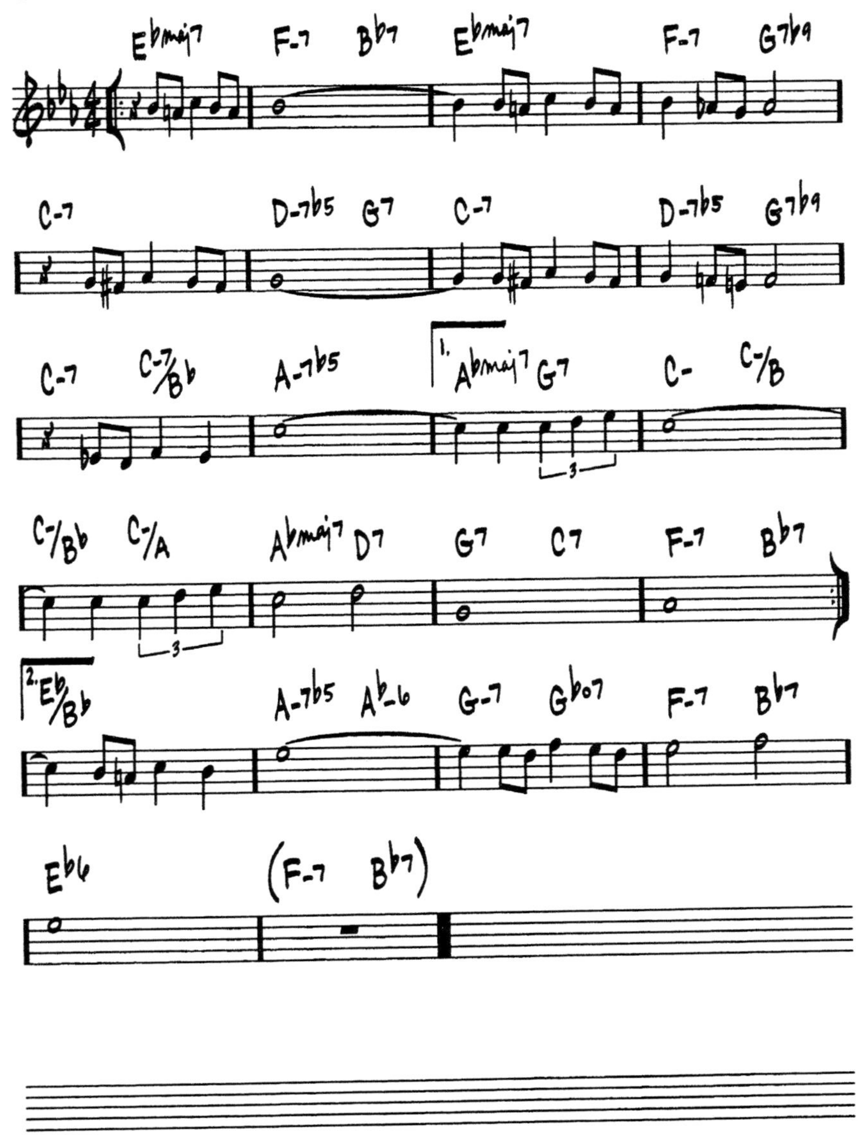

Copyright © 1929 (Renewed) by Chappell & Co.
Rights for the Extended Renewal Term in the U.S. Controlled by Williamson Music and WB Music Corp.
o/b/o The Estate Of Lorenz Hart

Copyright © 1929 Miller Music Corp. and Vincent Youmans, Inc.
Copyright Renewed and Assigned to Chappell & Co., WB Music Corp. and LSQ Music Co.

WORK SONG

(MED.)

-NAT ADDERLY/
OSCAR BROWN, JR.

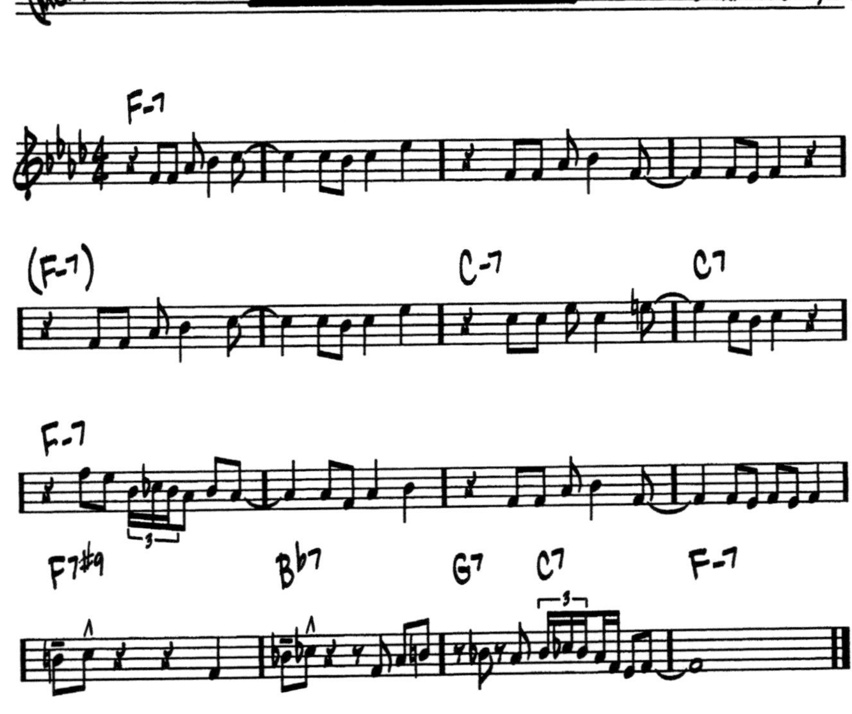

© 1960 (Renewed) by UPAM MUSIC CO., a division of Gopam Enterprises, Inc.

(BRIGHT) A WONDERFUL DAY LIKE TODAY

-LESLIE BRICUSSE/ANTHONY NEWLEY

Ebmaj7 Eb6 Ebmaj7 Eb6

Ebmaj7 Eb6 F-7 Bb7

F-7 Bb7 G-7 C7

1. Abmaj7 F7 F-7 Bb7

2. Abmaj7 F-7 Bb7 Eb6 F-7 F#o7 G7

Ab Ab+ Ab6 Ab7 Ao7

Ebmaj7 F-7 Bb7 Ebmaj7 Eb7

Abmaj7 A-7b5 D7b9

G-7 C7 F7 Bb7

© Copyright 1964 (Renewed) Concord Music Ltd., London, England
TRO - Musical Comedy Productions, Inc., New York, NY controls all publication rights for the U.S.A. and Canada

Ebmaj7 Eb6 Ebmaj7 Eb6
Ebmaj7 Eb6 F-7 Bb7
F-7 Bb7 G-7 C7
Abmaj7 G7 C-7 F7
F-7 Bb7 Eb6 (F-7 Bb7)

© 1956 (Renewed 1984) BEECHWOOD MUSIC CORP.

Copyright © 1946 (Renewed 1974) Atlantic Music Corp.

(MED. BALLAD)

YOU ARE BEAUTIFUL

-RICHARD RODGERS / OSCAR HAMMERSTEIN II

D6 C9 D6 C9

E-7 F#-7 Gmaj7 F#-7 |1. E-7 A7 D6 E-7 A7

|2. E-7 A7 A-7/D D7 Gmaj7 A7 B-7 D7/A

Gmaj7 A7 Dmaj7 D7 Gmaj7 F#7 B-7

E7 B-7 Bb7b5 A7 D6 C9

D6 C9 E-7 F#-7 Gmaj7 F#-7

E-7 A7 A-7 D7 Gmaj7 E-7 A7 A7b9

D6 (E-7 A7)

Copyright © 1958 by Richard Rodgers and Oscar Hammerstein II
Copyright Renewed
WILLIAMSON MUSIC owner of publication and allied rights throughout the world

Copyright © 1932 by Peer International Corporation
Copyright Renewed

(MED.)

YOU'D BE SO NICE TO COME HOME TO

—COLE PORTER

Copyright © 1942 by Chappell & Co.
Copyright Renewed, Assigned to Robert H. Montgomery, Trustee of the Cole Porter Musical and Literary Property Trusts
Chappell & Co. owner of publication and allied rights throughout the world

(MED.)

YOU'RE MY EVERYTHING

-HARRY WARREN/MORT DIXON/JOE YOUNG

Cmaj7 F#-7b5 B7 E-7 A7

D-7 G7

E-7 Eb-7 D-7 B-7b5 E7

A-7 D7 D-7 G7

Cmaj7 F#-7b5 B7 E-7 A7

D-7 B-7b5 E7

A-7 Ab7 G-7 C7 Fmaj7 F-6

E-7 Eb-7 D-7 G7 C6 (D-7 G7)

© 1931 WARNER BROS. INC.
© Renewed 1959 WAROCK CORP., OLDE CLOVER LEAF MUSIC and WARNER BROS. INC.
All Rights on behalf of OLDE CLOVER LEAF MUSIC Administered by FRED AHLERT MUSIC CORPORATION
Canadian rights controlled by WARNER BROS. INC.
All Rights Reserved

(Med.)

YOU'RE NOBODY 'TIL SOMEBODY LOVES YOU

-RUSS MORGAN/LARRY STOCK/JAMES CAVANAUGH

Gmaj7 B7 E7

A-7 D7 G6

B-7 B♭o7 A-7

A-7 A7 A-7 D7 A-7 D7

Gmaj7 B7 E7

A-7 E7 A- E7 A-

C C♯o7 Gmaj7 F♯7 F7 E7

A-7 A-7/D D7 G6 (E-7 A-7 D7)

Copyright © 1944 by Southern Music Pub. Co. Inc., Shapiro, Bernstein & Co., Inc. and Larry Stock Music Co. in the U.S.
Copyright Renewed

REAL BOOKS AVAILABLE

C, B♭, E♭ & Bass Clef Editons for:

The Real Book – Sixth Edition, Volume 1

The Real Book – Volume 2

The Real Book – Volume 3

More editions coming soon.

See your music dealer to order.

7777 W. BLUEMOUND RD. P.O. BOX 13819 MILWAUKEE, WI 53213

Visit Hal Leonard Online at
www.halleonard.com